The Golden Sands of Change

To order additional copies of this book, contact:
Xlibris
NZ TFN: 0800 008 756 (Toll Free inside the NZ)
NZ Local: 9-801 1905 (+64 9801 1905 from outside New Zealand)
www.xlibris.co.nz
Orders@ Xlibris.co.nz

ISBN: Softcover   978-1-6698-8047-9
        Hardcover   978-1-6698-8048-6
        EBook   978-1-6698-8046-2

Library of Congress Control Number: 2023905897

Print information available on the last page

Rev. date: 04/12/2023

Julia Giacomelli

The Golden Sands
of Change

A MEMOIR

To my family, the three of you who have built this life
with me: Franco, Jessica and Nathalie.
To the additional members who have joined us over the years: our sons-in-
law, and our grandchildren Oliver, Heidi, Phoebe, DeeDee and Rico.
And, of course, to my sister, Patricia, and her husband, Tony, and
to my brother, Malcolm, who is sadly no longer with us, and his
wife, Anita. Thank you for your unwavering support.

Contents

PART TWO

PART ONE

1

The Romance that Changed My Life

It's 1968, and I am crossing Europe, heading to Venice where I have agreed to marry a man I hardly know. I am twenty-three years old. The romance had started the previous year. We had met in London and began seeing each other quite regularly. Franco, however, was called home to Venice as his father had died. Now he had to return to help with a family business. We exchanged contact details. Since I was waiting for my sister, Patricia, to join me in London – we had planned a tour of Europe together – it was easy to agree to call in on him on our return from Greece.

Patricia and I continued our tour and agreed to allow a little more time in Venice. Our plans all fell into place. On arrival in Venice, we parked the car at Piazzale Roma, the last point before you encounter the challenge of the Venetian public transport boats. We found a small hotel very close to Piazza San Marco, St Mark's Square, referred to as la Piazza by the locals, and soon headed into the square – the Ballroom of Europe, as it has been called. There we met up with both Franco and Roberto, one of his London friends.

We did all our sightseeing by day, and at night we went dancing in some of the most beautiful ballrooms I have ever seen. I learnt a little more about this new friend of mine. He spoke five languages and was the most amazing dancer. I had done competitive ballroom and Latin dancing in my teens and appreciated his skill. It was all starting to take on a dream-like quality – the time I spent with Franco, our budding relationship, and my stay in Venice.

We sadly said our farewells and Patricia and I returned to London. While in London, I shared a flat with a lovely English friend, Judy. Patricia was staying on in London, while I was heading home to New Zealand. The next few days were spent packing and preparing for the flight home. I made one last visit to our relations in Kent. Returning to the flat, it was a very wet and cold London night. I walked in the door, sniffing and complaining, to see Judy sat up looking very prim and proper, knees together, with a book open in her hands. Judy appeared a little puzzled. As I entered the lounge, Franco was stood behind the door. He had driven the entire journey from Venice to London, non-stop. He had three friends with him, and they only had a few days in London.

The following days were rather strange. He and I talked so much, and plans started to take shape. I would return to Venice … we could get married … We talked about family, the difference in lifestyle between Venice and what I was accustomed to, and similar topics – all concerning us having a life together. It was agreed I should still return to New Zealand, and once at home, I should tell the family about our intentions, then return to Venice towards the end of the year. The decision made, he drove non- stop back to Venice and went straight to work.

Back home in New Zealand, telling the family of our plans was not as easy as anticipated, and every reason as to why I should not return to Venice to be with Franco was on the daily agenda. My father tried to suggest I would be living in a gondola and eating fish all day. I am allergic to fish! Good try, Dad! Eventually, they suggested he should come to New Zealand. Franco replied that he would be out to visit me at the end of the Italian summer. My parents then decided that if Franco was going to set up a new life with me, he would need all his money. So they decided they would bring their overseas trip forward, and within a week they had set off to tour Europe and would be in Venice later in the year to meet Franco. I started making preparation to return to Venice. In those days, young women saved household items in a glory box – a hope chest or trousseau – for the day they were married. Useful things, such as bed linen, table linen, fine dishes, clothes, and so on, were lovingly placed inside. I filled my trunk with books! I knew I would have to learn a new language and would not have many friends, so books were going to save the day.

The day I got off the train at the Venezia Santa Lucia railway station, near the western end of the Grand Canal in Venice, the sun was shining, the Grand Canal was sparkling, and the magnificent Church of Madonna della Salute was breathtaking. It all felt so good and so right; this was going to be my home.

Franco arranged a private *motoscafo*, the smaller launches that are the taxis of Venice, to take us home to the Lido di Venezia, Venice Lido, an island in the Venetian lagoon. A canal ran just a few steps from the front door of his family's home. Some very grumpy helpers managed to get my chest of books off the boat. The family's villa was surrounded by a huge brick wall with an iron gate set in it. Spikes of broken glass topped the wall, leading me to wonder whether this island was a safe place to live. I was very nervous about entering his home. I knew he was living alone with his mother, since his four older siblings, three sisters and a brother, were all married and living away. This was the beginning of the 'dry gum' era in my life. If you can't understand a word being spoken, you simply smile, and at the end of the day there is no moisture left in your mouth!

2

The Wedding

TWENTIETH OF OCTOBER 1968

Plans for the wedding were underway. Franco's sister Lilly (Lilliana) became the commander-in-chief and did a wonderful job of making the arrangements. All the details were attended to, and given my inability to speak Italian, agreements were either sealed in sign language or by dragging Franco into the negotiations. He almost did a walkout, though, when it came to a new bra that I needed for my wedding gown. I had asked him to meet me at the lingerie shop. Due to a lack of space, every item was tucked away in a draw, and the customer had to tell the shop assistant their bra size. In Italy, this involves only the chest measurement, whereas in New Zealand we include the cup size. Although I was very slim, I did have an abundant cup size. I heard him say something about a 'soup bowl' size, and I became rather emotional. Offended, I walked out in tears. They chased me down the street. On our return to the shop, the dear lady guided me into the dressing room, took some measurements, and all was well. I wasn't surprised that Franco wanted to rush back to work; it was not exactly a great lunch break.

Luck was on my side the day an English-speaking priest was called in to hear my confession before the wedding. Fortunately, his English might have been six words at best, so I was able to make a clean breast of it. In truth, I could have been responsible for some ghastly murder and got away with it.

The magnificent church at which we were married was Sant Antonio di Padova on the Lido. Built in 1936 in a Veneto-Byzantine style, it is as large as a cathedral. It was glorious on our wedding day, filled with a mass of flowers, music and light. I sincerely thanked Lilly, my new sister- in-law, for her efforts.

The reception was at one of the family's hotels. The restaurant had been beautifully decorated, with the tables set for Italian-speaking guests on one side, and English-speaking guests on the other. A huge amount of smiling, waving, shouting and general good cheer ensued across the divide. We could only laugh when attempts at translating went badly wrong, followed by repeated attempts at corrections and then more laughter. It did take a while for common understanding to be established, but the enthusiasm of the participants could not be faulted.

We were due to travel up to the Dolomite Mountains for the first stop of our honeymoon, our wedding night. What was not relayed to me was that almost the entire family would be there, too.

Franco's older brother, Berto, and his older sister, Elda, ran the hotel in Rolle, and since Berto could not get to the wedding due to work commitments, his sister Lilly and his mother decided to have a break up there at the same time. We spent a couple of days at the hotel, enjoying the spectacular Dolomites, also known as the 'Pale Mountains', which comprise a great many ranges. Then we left for Pisa and Florence.

On our return to Venice, la Signora was back home. Franco went to work, and my new mother-in-law and I had time to get to know each other. It went badly wrong one day when she kept pointing to my feet and shouting. I thought I had spilt water on her special marble floors. At a certain point she phoned Franco at work, then handed the phone to me. The outcome was that I had bare feet (as we often do when indoors in New Zealand), and she was trying to tell me I would catch a chill in my kidneys. Dear lady. We had a hug and carried on.

Lido was starting to feel more friendly. With less tourists bustling about, the shop owners started to recognise me as one of their own. Franco would give me a shopping list of what was required. The shop owners would make me pronounce the item's name in Italian then check it off against Franco's list. Peals of laughter (friendly, mind you, always friendly) would ring out, then they'd start again by telling me the word's correct pronunciation. Finally, the purchase would be made. Obviously, my shopping excursions must have been a giggle a minute for them, but eventually I decided to save the week's shopping for the markets that came to the Lido on Tuesdays.

The markets opened at 5.30 am, but by 8 am were so packed as to be hazardous. All the shoppers dragged little shopping trolleys behind them, which became lethal weapons if you were not aware of them and quick to step aside. As the food was cheaper at the markets, they were always packed and an absolute scramble. The shouting and shoving started when the shoppers pushed in and vied to catch the eye of the market stall keeper to be served next. Watching for their turn, they all talked, shouted and laughed with gusto. Just when it began to sound like a punch-up was imminent, the culprits would suddenly break into laugher.

Quietly, I would stand and wait, and I would put my hand up from time to time. Fortunately, there was always some dear person who would grab my arm, yell at the others, and say it was the turn of *la donna Inglese*, the English woman. Each word that came out of my mouth became a real competitive challenge for the shoppers as they all tried to guess what I was saying. Toilet paper was my worst nightmare. You can only do so many ladylike hand movements to indicate you wanted to purchase this product. They loved the guessing game and fell about laughing once we all understood what I was after.

3

Carnevale di Venezia, Farewell to Meat

It is accepted that the first Carnevale di Venezia, the Carnival of Venice, was held in Venice in 1094. It is an annual event, held as a celebration preceding the forty days of Lent, since the latter involves abstinence and penitence. The Carnival ends on Shrove Tuesday, the day before the start of Lent on Ash Wednesday. The idea among Venetians during the time before Lent is, *Let's have the biggest party we can!* Since the earliest celebration of the Carnival, the festivities included minstrels, actors, competitions, balls, banquets, and pageantry.

The great Grand Lords of Fun introduced the wearing of masks very early on in the tradition. The idea being that a Grand Lord should dress as a servant, and for everyone to have a different identity. Of course, the freedom to misbehave was a key factor. The tradition of Carnival flourished, and by the 18th century it reached the height of its splendour. The annual celebration of the Carnival was outlawed in 1797, and the use of masks became strictly forbidden. This situation coincided with the foreign domination of Venice at the hands of Napoleon Bonaparte, and then Habsburg Austria. Napoleon, in particular, thought the entire festival was a security risk.

For nearly two hundred years minor efforts were made to bring the festival back, with some small success in the 19th century, but only for short periods and largely as limited private affairs. The Church and the Communists, however, condemned lavish parties and the Carnival slept again until 1950, when modest, mostly private events started up again. After a long absence, the Carnival proper, as a public celebration, returned in 1979.

The Carnival in modern times is a combination of folklore and history, with a touch of Disneyland. Since its revival, a huge stage is erected in Piazza San Marco for the best masked-costume competition. Venetians and their children come to see and be seen. At dusk the costumed contenders promenade through the arches, allowing themselves to be admired and photographed. The children have a wonderful time. Since it is a very cold month, keeping the children warm under such lavish attire is a real challenge. In the 18th century, visitors were amazed that up to thirty thousand people would attend Carnevale di Venezia. In recent years, before the Covid-19 epidemic, more than a hundred thousand people have been recorded in Piazza San Marco in one afternoon.

During my first experience of Carnival, as the evening drew in, the little ones went home, and the fit, healthy and naughty stayed on to celebrate, dressed exactly as they did in the 18th century. Attendees were masked most of the time, but naturally, we all took a peep to make sure we were in our own group. Well, at least most of us did. The world's greatest ballroom became a blaze of light. The columns along the square were all backlit to spectacular effect. Saint Mark's Basilica was illuminated to reveal almost every stone, probably as a subtle reminder of the type of behaviour expected! Three orchestras took turns to keep the music flowing.

As with all festivals, the older people had their own way of joining in. My mother-in-law told me of the custom in her day when all the 'housewives' would take a kitchen chair and a cushion, and their sewing or crocheting, and sit on the edge of the island along the Grand Canal during Carnevale and watch the comings and goings of the costumed revellers. Grown-ups who were slightly inebriated when they landed on the jetty, were a particular source of amusement to them. It must have been a fun night for all involved.

There were and still are numerous shops throughout Venice that supply only costumes and masks. In fact, these shops are extremely popular and are packed with a huge selection of wares. The same applies to costume experts, both those who design and craft bespoke items and those who offer off-the-shelf options. The latter do enormous trade, even with the tourists of today. We purchased outfits for our two girls quite regularly, because each year the girls would have grown a little and alterations were not always feasible. Some swapping and exchanging of costumes among friends took place, of course, because their children had grown too, and most outfits did not fit the following year. Part of the excitement and fun for our children, leading up to and during Carnival, was being on the ferry boat going into Venice, and seeing all their friends. We mums would hang out together and keep a watchful eye on the children.

4

Summer in Venice

SUMMER ON THE BEACH

With the start of summer, we all had a completely new wardrobe. Winter clothes were cleaned and packed away, and out came sandals, summer dresses, shorts, designer swimwear, and so on. The entire population of Venice looked elegant and refreshed. We all went off to the cabanas on the Lido beaches on the eastern side of the island, facing the Adriatic Sea. Its western side borders the Venetian Lagoon.

The Lido is famous not only for its natural beaches but also for its luxury hotels. Along the kilometres of pale golden sand, sections are separated off in front of each hotel, starting at the top end with the Grand Hotel Des Bains, inaugurated in 1900, all the way to the other end. These beaches have been used by the rich and famous from around the world since the 1800s. For the less affluent, there are large public beaches towards the northern and southern ends of the Lido, also characterised by the pale golden sand dunes.

We were fortunate to join the family in their *tukul* on the beach at the Des Bains. A *tukul* resembles a straw-roofed hut, very similar to the ones you see in Africa. The beach at Des Bains had a beautiful restaurant and bar for refreshments and waiters who attend to guests as required. We swam, dined, sunbathed, and chatted all day. The beaches opened in June and closed on 15 September. While the men were at work, my sister-in- law Lilly and my mother in-law, along with the little ones, enjoyed these visits to the beach all summer long.

My girlfriends and I would take turns going to one another's beach cabanas, which, of course, were not strictly ours but rather the property of our husbands' families. They booked these cabanas year after year, usually the same one each time. Some people would take their own lunch to their beach cabanas, while others would just pop into the hotel's bar for something to eat. Since each beach had its own restaurant and bars attached to the hotel along that section of the shore, we again enjoyed long lunches during the heat of the day. At the end of a day spent on the beach during the working week, we would meet the husbands as they stepped off the boat, dash down to the shops to pick up some wine and food, and then carry on relaxing on the beach as the sun set over Venice. On the weekends, when the husbands were free to join the women and children on the beach, we enjoyed long lunches, either on the beach or in one of the bars or restaurants close by, which often carried on into the late evening.

We used this time to talk about the day, swim (there were no sharks) and, of course, sing. These were wonderful summers. Even though we discussed politics quite a lot during the evenings, we were miserably unable to get through to the people who mattered and had no influence on them in this regard.

Again, for me, this stage in the annual cycle of life in Venice was new, and therefore accompanied by a new vocabulary that I had to contend with. The Italians in each region have their own dialect, but most of the time they speak to their children in standard Italian, and in the local dialect to one another, which for us was Venetian. I tried to speak to the children in Italian, which, though entertaining to them, meant that we did not make progress in understanding one another. I tried communicating with them in English, but it was considered not a good idea as it would confuse the little ones!

THE PASSEGGIATA

For Venetians, the daily walk, the *passeggiata*, is the event of the day in summertime. To me the idea of simply walking – if not for exercise – seemed bizarre. To the Italians, it was all about one's social life and it attracted its own etiquette. First of all, you are expected to really dress up, you are not to be in shorts or a T-shirt, since the elegance of those promenading about is to be noted and admired. There were about fifty bars, cafés and restaurants on the Lido where you could sit *al fresco*. People were inclined to use the same bar every day, so if you had a special friend and you wanted to catch up with only that person, you wouldn't go to your crowd's usual bar because then you would be involved in conversations with everyone else and have little privacy. Even the elderly had their hotspots. You would see older men walking arm in arm, as did the women. Some had their favourite table, which you got to recognise, and you would move along to give them their space when they arrived.

At the bars and cafés along the route of your passeggiata, there were always an enormous selection of ice creams and a plethora of drinks representing almost every nationality. On one occasion, on our return to Lido after being away in New Zealand, we bumped into a couple of Franco's old mates. We sat down and ordered an aperitif. In a short time, more friends stopped by, saying, "Hey, it's Giacomelli!" Soon a crowd congregated, all people who knew one another, and they filled the entire side of the street, extending well beyond the actual bar where we were seated. It finished up being a party. This would have been at about three in the afternoon.

No matter what time of the day, these places were always busy. For breakfast, the counters were full of tasty croissants, beautiful tramezzini (large, triangular club sandwiches), which were my favourite. Cakes, custard squares, a veritable banquet was on display. If you were off to work, you would eat at the bar, with an espresso to accompany your breakfast. But if you were joining a friend, you would sit at a table, and you could spend all morning there if you had a lot to talk about.

In the summer, everyone was out and about on their bicycles. It was convenient; you can hang a huge number of plastic shopping bags on the handlebars and still keep going. If required, you could still stop on the side of the road and have a chat. The scooters in contrast, were noisy, and there were literally hundreds of them.

Another interesting observation was the number of older men sitting in bars at ten in the morning. They would talk and play cards and have a drink, often times of the non-alcoholic sort, or simply wile away the hours relaxing. The elderly men were out at this time of day mainly because the Italian housewife will not have a man round her feet while she is doing her household chores. The beds were stripped down to the mattress daily, and the sheets would be flapping from the balcony, getting a good airing in the breeze, and when all was just as it should be in the home, the woman of the house would dress up and go to meet hubby in the bar. There they would enjoy an *aperitivo* and then visit the markets or shops to pick up the daily shopping. By the time they got home, their entire social life would have been updated.

CONCERTS IN THE PIAZZA

During the summer months we had a period of cultural experiences in the Piazza San Marco. Not only has St Mark's Square been called the Ballroom of Europe, but Napoleon also called it "the finest drawing room in Europe". Both of which often seemed to be total understatements because the Italians have the magic touch when it comes to putting on a show.

Spectacular outdoor shows in Venice started with a free Pink Floyd concert in 1989, which turned out to be a disaster for the city. The band performed on a floating stage on the Grand Canal next to St Mark's Square. The crowds were unbelievable, with 200 thousand attending. There was insufficient space, too few toilets, and inadequate rubbish disposal. Consequently, the event ruined so much of the magical 'drawing room' ambience of la Piazza. People were climbing up the ancient columns of the arcades, destroying the delicate, intricate filigree of the stone carvings. We didn't go to this concert, but the horror and destruction almost stopped the city of Venice from ever allowing another event of this nature.

The Venetian residents, however, were very vocal, you could say almost impossible to shut up. (Thank goodness.) Since then, we have seen some beautiful expressions of unbelievable talent during events held al fresco in la Piazza. We attended a performance by the American Ballet, with Mikhail Baryshnikov and Gelsey Kirkland headlining, for instance. The stage backdrop was the Piazza's rows of beautiful columns and distinctive architecture. It was a stage setting not to be missed and never to be forgotten. We were able to experience amazing performances of symphony music, ballet, theatre and opera in this incredible 'drawing room'. Not to forget that it was also very much our local after-work pub!

VENICE HISTORICAL REGATTA

Every first Sunday in September, one of the oldest and biggest events in Venice, the Regata Storica di Venezia, the Venice Historical Regatta, a colourful historic water pageant, is held in the Venetian Lagoon. Since the earliest days of Venice, Venetians have been organising boat races, and these were later transformed into organised regattas. Some of the earliest evidence about such races dates back to the 13th century and refers to events associated with the Festa delle Marie, which itself originated in the 10th century. Historical documents record, for instance, that in January 1315 a regatta was held, but races of this size and pomp were subsequently held only to celebrate military victories or to honour important foreign dignitaries.

The Historical Regatta as we know it, appears to have started in the 15th century to commemorate the welcome given to Caterina Cornaro in 1489, when, after marrying the King of Cyprus, she refused the throne, giving it up in favour of Venice.

During the Regatta, the ancient barges that belonged to the doge (the head of state, somewhat similar to a duke, almost royalty) are prepared and launched to recall and display all the glamour and glory of the past. The formal part of the Regatta is a historical parade along the entire length of the Grand Canal, beginning at Piazza San Marco, with all the fanfare and theatre the Italians do so well. The parade also features traditional Venetian boats and gondolas. These are all crewed and occupied by people from the different Venetian rowing associations dressed in local historical costumes, enacting their roles from the past. The parade is followed by the different categories of races for various age groups and types of vessels, and between all sorts of rowing boats from many different countries. These vessels range from small, two person or even single rowboats, to the great English rowing teams of Oxford and Cambridge. Women compete, as do business enterprises and sports clubs. The list of competitors is never-ending. The highlight of the Regatta is the race between *gondolini a due remi* These are extremely light, narrow and fast gondolas powered by one man with two oars.

One year Franco was rowing for Team Alitalia, with Team British Airways hot on their tail. To say that this event in September was a great party is an understatement. The entire city and its islands were having a massive party, from one end to the other. Toward evening, an exhausted husband arrived home to collapse on the couch.

It wasn't long before all the other rowers in his team were showered and changed, and they turned up looking for him to party. We managed to get him sorted and out the door. We all went to celebrate and party, along with every single Venetian who could stand upright, at least sufficiently to celebrate.

Pink Floyd concert in Piazza San Marco

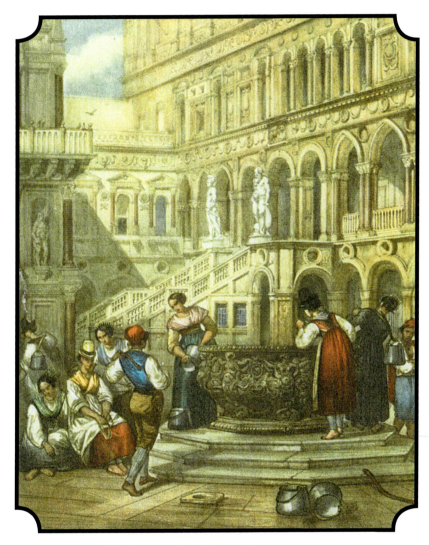

Daily gossip while collecting water

5

Snippets of History

A BRIEF HISTORY OF VENICE

Tradition has it that Venice was founded in AD 421, with a church being established on Rialto. At that time, a Celtic people, the Veneti, who had been Roman citizens since 49 BC, lived along the coast of what is now north-eastern Italy. When Attila the Hun invaded Italy in 453, some Veneti fled to islands in the Venetian Lagoon and built a village there. They soon formed a loose federation, and the Venetian Islands were flourishing in the time of the Roman Empire. Then in 568, a people called the Lombards invaded the mainland, and many Veneti fled to the islands, increasing the population.

The Republic of Venice, known as 'la Serenissima', was founded in 697, after the decline of the Roman Empire, by people escaping from Germanic invasions. At first, Venice was controlled by the Byzantine Empire. The office of doge goes back to 697, when the Republic was founded, and the seat of government was on the island of Malamocco (now the Lido). In 726, Orso Ipato led a revolt against the Byzantine Empire and the Venetians partly gained their independence, but they continued to follow a Byzantine system of administration. In the same year they elected Orso Ipato as the third doge of Venice but also the first historical *Venetian* doge.

The Franks tried but failed to conquer the Venetians in 810. In the same year the seat of the duchy moved to the area of Rivoalto (the present-day Rialto), and it was a time of greater autonomy for Venice and the beginning of her history of constructing beautiful buildings. In 820, the seat moved to the main island of Venice, San Marco, where it was to remain. Venice continued to flourish as a port and a trading centre, gaining advantage as the trading intermediary between two great empires: the Byzantine Empire and the Western Empire.

Those deciding to settle in Venice adapted to the sea environment, creating thriving urban settlements and lines of communication between the many islands. The bonds between the Venetian Islands became stronger and stronger through the centuries. The islands had a significant strategic function in protecting Venice from tides and foreign invaders. Monasteries and convents were established on the islands and became centres of worship, culture and knowledge. Hospitals and a mental institution were established on the islands.

In the Middle Ages, Venice continued to prosper as a port and trading centre. Ships sailed from San Nicolo on the Lido for the Crusades and pilgrimage to the Holy Land, and on trade voyages to the East.

The Venetians persuaded the Crusaders of the failed Eleventh Crusade, who could not pay for the ships the Venetians had built for them, to join them in an expedition to raid Constantinople. The city was subsequently captured and looted in 1204. Venice was also involved in other wars at that time. The city of Genoa was a powerful rival to Venice and from the late 13th century onward, for nearly two centuries, Venice and Genoa were periodically at war, fighting five wars in total.

Over the centuries that followed, the Republic of Venice dominated the trade routes on the Mediterranean Sea, from Asia to Africa. It became a rich merchant republic as well as a leading military power whose territories spread from northern Italy to Greece.

The Black Death devastated the population of Venice in 1348, and therefore, in 1403, Venice introduced a period of *quarantina giorni* (forty days) to help control the plague and other epidemics. Ships arriving from infected areas had to anchor at one of the *lazzaretti*, quarantine stations, built on three of the islands, and the passengers had to wait for forty days, that is, be quarantined, before they were allowed to enter the city. The sick in the city were also sent there.

In the 15th century Venice faced a new threat – the Turks, as they encroached on the Byzantine Empire in the East. Peace with the Turks was finally achieved in 1479. The Venetians, though, soon became involved in another war, this time with Ferrara, as the Italian states increasingly opposed Venice's territorial expansion.

From the 16th century onward, the Venetians invested heavily in the purchase, reclamation, and drainage of *terraferma* (dry lands). In 1508, several European countries, including the Spanish, French, Germans, Hungarians, Savoyards, and Ferrarese, together with the pope, united to form the League of Cambrai and went to war against Venice. The war lasted eight years but it left the Venetian territories virtually unchanged. In 1630 the plague struck Venice again.

During the 17th century, Venice gradually lost power and influence. In the 18th century, Venice was not an important player politically, although the arts flourished. The Republic of Venice lasted more than a millennium until 1797, when Napoleon dissolved it. After his fall in 1815, Venice was handed to Hapsburg Austria. Venice did not prosper under Austrian rule, and in 1848 Venice rose in rebellion against Austria, but was forced to surrender in August 1849. After the Prussians defeated Austria in 1866, Venice was ceded to Italy, which had been a united kingdom since 1861. In the late 19th century, Venice flourished as a port and a manufacturing centre. Now, the lands once owned by Venice belong to seven different countries: Italy, Slovenia, Croatia, Montenegro, Albania, Greece and Cyprus.

LIDO DI VENEZIA

With my new bike, I decided to tour and study the beautiful island where we lived, Lido di Venezia, which I felt had been gifted to me. The Lido, one of the 118 islands comprising Venice, is a barrier island only 11 kilometres long and 700 metres at its widest point, covering an area of 4 square kilometres. It protects the Venetian Lagoon from the Adriatic Sea on the eastern side, and, as mentioned, this shoreline has a series of beautiful long, wide, sandy beaches. The western side faces toward Venice, the Venetian Lagoon, and the mainland of Italy.

On clear days, the view with the Dolomite Mountains behind the city's towers and rooftops, and all the lovely islands in between, is incredible. It is also a picture that changes with sunrise and sunset.

The Lido di Venezia was initially farmland with gardens, vineyards, stables, canals, windmills, and wells located near military fortifications that made up part of the Lagoon's ancient defence system. But the island renewed itself in the 19th and early 20th century, becoming *the* sought- after summer holiday resort for the European aristocracy and the rich and famous. The rural landscape was gradually replaced with eclectically designed villas and hotels.

While there are roads on the Lido, canals criss-cross the island and barges deliver all manner of goods to the locals – food, water, wine, household goods, furniture, petrol, and so forth. The island has bus and taxi services, and emergency services such as an ambulance and fire brigade. The main street, the Gran Viale Santa Maria Elisabetta, runs across the island from the Adriatic beaches on the eastern side, to the stop for the *vaporetti* (the larger water buses) on the Lagoon on the western side. Even though the Lido is the only Venetian Island that allows bikes, pedal cars, and motorised traffic, the stunning villas, unique architecture, exquisite gardens, floral decorations, beautiful willows, and the diverse styles of the bridges connecting it all, made our regular passeggiatta a delight.

Over the years the history and architecture on the island, with its churches, art deco buildings, and magnificent Belle Époque- and Liberty- style villas, accumulated, and it could take a lifetime to study. Small and compact, a sense of mystery lingers on every gateway and doorway on the island.

The Lido's lovely old parish church, Santa Maria Elisabetta, small and demure, just seems to sit there and watch the chaos all around. Built in the mid-16th century as an oratory, then enlarged and converted into a church in 1627, it was consecrated in 1671. Extensive restoration work was done to it around 1970. It was the place of worship for the first vine growers, the island's first inhabitants. At that time, the church was close to the Lagoon's western bank, as shown in a drawing by Canaletto (*Venice: Sant'Elena from San Pietro, c. 1740*). With the natural shifting of the sandbank, the church is more inland in the present day.

The other notable historic building, further along the edge of the Lagoon, is Santa Maria della Vittoria. Built in 1925 to 1938 as a memorial to the Italian dead of the First World War, it is also known as the Venice War Memorial and the Tempio Votivo. The circular structure's shape was inspired by art nouveau and designed by U. V. Fantucci, while its large green dome was designed by Giuseppe Torres. It is one of the first landmarks seen as you approach the Lido vaporetti stop.

In addition to these islands, there is also Murano, known worldwide as the glassblowing island; it is where all the amazing hand-blown glass is made. The island of Burano, known as one of the most colourful places in the world, is famous for its fishing and needle-lace making. Burano is still producing a vast range of exquisite pieces today.

SAN MICHELE ISLAND

Isola di San Michele is known as the Cemetery Island in Venice. It was originally two smaller, separate islands, San Michele and San Cristoforo della Pace, which were artificially joined when the canal that separated the two islands was filled in during 1836. San Cristoforo was selected to become a cemetery in 1807, when Napoleon instructed the Venetians to stop burying their dead within the city, and construction of its beautiful monumental cemetery began the same year.

The island was named for the existing church, Chiesa di San Michele in Isola, the Church of San Michele (on the Island), dedicated to the Archangel Michael. It was designed in 1469 by the famous architect Mauro Codussi and was the first Renaissance church in Venice. The island has several magnificent churches and chapels, including the Chapel of San Rocco, the Church of San Cristoforo, and the Emiliani Chapel, which is attached to the Church of San Michele.

The Monastery of San Michele, originally built in the 10th century, was rebuilt in the mid-1400s. The monastery consisted of ancient cloisters, the dormitory of the Camaldolese monks, the Church of San Michele, and, of course, the cemetery. The old monastery also served for a time as a prison! The vineyards of San Michele are in the novices' garden of the monastery, which is near the cemetery. The monastery has been managed for the past two centuries by the Franciscan friars.

A high, red-brick wall surrounds the island, with the imposing landing and gates of San Michele Cemetery being especially impressive. Within the enclosed area lies the monastery and the cemetery with its gardens and their tall, sombre cypresses. The cemetery is divided into sections, according to Christian denomination: Catholic, Orthodox and Evangelical, and other criteria, such as Commonwealth War Dead and even gondoliers. Besides notable Venetians, many other well-known people are buried there, including Joseph Brodsky, Sergei Diaghilev, Igor Stravinsky and Ezra Pound, to mention but a few names that may be more familiar to non-Italians.

To travel between the islands, the most convenient forms of public transport are the local motoscafo and *piccola* (small) motoscafo, which run like clockwork. If the timetable indicates the arrival or departure to be four minutes past the hour, that is exactly the time it will turn up. If any boat is even two minutes late, the locals are almost beside themselves with concern! There is also the local water taxi service, which is quite upmarket with nice upholstery and plenty of room and has the advantage of being able to take you right to your door.

6

End of Summer

CHANGE OF SEASON

As the end of summer came round, there were fewer and fewer tourists in Venice, and the beaches on the Lido closed on 15 September. This was the signal for each household to undertake preparations for the *cambio (di stagione),* the change (of season). From every balcony you could see beach towels, summer clothes, bed linen, duvet covers, and so forth, washed and hung out to air. For almost a week, you would imagine, the basis of each household's activities was hanging out and taking in laundry. Out came the heavier jackets, leather and otherwise. The men changed the weight of their trousers, handbag styles changed, and we all looked like a completely different crowd. In fact, the Venetians were absolutely right to do so, because although there was only a slight change in temperature, and the odd cloud may have appeared, it definitely was cambio di stagione. In our variable climate in New Zealand, we usually had all our options of clothing, footwear, and bed linen out most of the time since our weather changes each day. Anyway, follow your neighbour was the rule. I made all the correct changes, and all was well.

Christmas was around the corner and the lights in Piazza San Marco were like a fairy-tale wonderland. When we lived in Venice, quite often we would all gather there to experience the special charm of the Christmas season. True to its name, the Ballroom of Europe, many groups would form in la Piazza to enjoy and admire the Christmas decorations. When you saw your group of friends or family, you simply joined them. The group could finish up with more than twenty convivial people. For the Venetians, St Mark's Square is their meeting room; they have a real need to talk and exchange ideas and opinions. Politics, the economy, gossip, world affairs, health and medicine — it was all open for discussion. If these subjects were of no interest to you, you were free to just tag along to the next group. There was always someone you knew in the group. If you wanted a top-up of your drink, you just popped into the nearest bar. There were several we could use right on la Piazza. Simply pick up a glass of wine and tell them that Franco G. would pay. No problem, everyone knew who he was. The locals all knew one another, and this quaint commercial arrangement seemed to work well.

The journey home from the Christmas drinks and chats was on one of the *motornavi* (the foot-passenger ferries for carrying large numbers of passengers and used on the longer routes) that run from

Lido to Venice and back all the time. It, too, had a bar and there was always a risk that 'one for the road' was on the way and could not be declined. Strangely, in those days there was no bad behaviour on board. The vessel's entire crew and passengers were locals. Still, I don't have an update on how their livers function today, but the effect of the over-indulgence probably has them better off than they would have been with the road rage and traffic jams they would have had to endure in other cities.

To celebrate Christmas Mass, Franco took me to the Church of the Heart of Jesus, on Via Navarrino, on the Lido. It is at the monastery of a cloistered order of nuns, le Suore Bianche, the White Nuns, which also houses their convent. They are properly called *Figlie del Cuore di Gesù. I*n English, the Daughters of the Heart of Jesus. During Mass, the nuns were all sequestered behind huge iron gates; we could only see their backs. The church, of red-brick and faintly Gothic in structure, was very plainly finished with a total absence of decoration. But I have to say, it was the most beautiful choir I have ever listened to.

With the cold weather approaching, calm descended on the Lido as the manic rush of tourists dramatically decreased. Although, all the local businesses did need tourism to sustain commerce. The Lido, along with its inhabitants, were now dressed for winter, and we witnessed the March of the Bears, as I initially called them. Almost everyone wore a fur coat, and every possible animal was represented on the street as a garment or as footwear: leather boots, leather gloves. I already had a pair of lovely leather gloves, purchased in Florence on our honeymoon. After a very short time, however, I stopped my silly comments and graciously accepted a beautiful white lapin fur coat and an amazing pair of leather boots. The thick fog, the rain, and the cold weather generally, meant a genuine need for protection against the elements. (Or so I told myself.) I think it was only a year later that the Animal Rights movements came into play, and many placed their fur and animal skin garments in storage.

ACQUA ALTA

In late autumn, the Acqua Alta (the high water), caused by storm surges from the Adriatic Sea or by heavy rain, come to Venice. When the sirens wail in the middle of the night, residents go through the usual routine of barricading their homes, restaurants, and places of business with sandbags to protect them from the high winds and flooding waters.

The Piazza San Marco is not far above sea level and is quick to flood. Winds whip up waves in the submerged square and crash the gondolas into quays and bridges. After the infamous Acqua Alta flood in 1966, the cost of the repair to St Marks Basilica was estimated to be close to two million euros.

One year a motoscafo was pushed right into the Piazzetta di San Marco, an adjoining open space connecting the south side of the Piazza San Marco to the waterway of the Lagoon. The Piazzetta lies between the Doge's Palace on the east, and Jacopo Sansovino's Biblioteca (Library) on the west. The water swept the motoscafo clean across the Molo, the quay fronting the Lagoon at the end of the piazzetta.

When we heard the flood sirens one year – it was 1968 – we did what seemed the right thing to do in the middle of the night and went out to see what was happening on the Lido. Launches were crushed under bridges or into people's garden walls. In one case, three were tangled together in a mess.

We climbed the Murazzi, a complex of massive stone seawalls and dams built since the end of 18th century on the Adriatic side to defend the Lagoon's inhabited areas against sea erosion and to protect it from the Adriatic's surges during Acqua Alta. The Murazzi are divided into three sections, the first being at the Lido. In November 1966, their failure was one of the causes of the exceptional high water that flooded the city of Venice. At the Murazzi there were many people milling about, all checking up on their losses with despair.

Today huge gates called the MOSE (Experimental Electromechanical Module) have been built to protect Venice from the problem of flooding. While an impressive feat of engineering, the entire project has been fraught with delays, corruption, and general maladministration.

The consensus seems to be that the system is working. When you think that almost all the buildings in Venice have a ground floor locked off because it cannot be made dry enough to inhabit, the very real consequences of flooding are put into perspective. Despite the mass exodus from the city core of Venice to the mainland, a shortage of affordable housing exists. Venetians on the main islands have to deal with old, decaying and often damp buildings, their rents inflated by the costs of renovation, the tourist market, and wealthy foreign residents – whose dwellings remain empty for most of the year. Venetians have moved, in growing numbers, into modern apartments on the mainland or on the Lido, where accommodation is also in very short supply. Venice continues to be a very expensive city in which to live. Hopefully, Venice has done battle for the last time, with yet another enemy determined to destroy its magic – the Acqua Alta.

Is Venice sinking? Yes, without a doubt. The cost and effort required to constantly maintain and rebuild the support structures for not only the houses people live in, but also the major historic buildings, churches and cathedrals, and the exquisite bridges, is enormous. And that is not even to mention the care and funds required to preserve the lovely islands, and the great works by the masters of art.

Armenian Island

7

The Armenian Island and the Lazzaretto Islands

THE ARMENIAN ISLAND OF SAINT LAZARUS

From the small bridge near our apartment on the Lido, on the Lagoon side, we could see isola di San Lazzaro degli Armeni, the island of Saint Lazarus of the Armenians, or Saint Lazarus Island, also known among the locals as 'the Armenian Island'. It has a prime location in the Venetian Lagoon – behind the San Marco Basin and the island of San Giorgio, placing it close to the heart of Venice and to the island of Lido. The monastery island is named after St Lazarus, the patron saint of lepers. One of the first diseases coming to Venice from the East was leprosy, and the island was a leper colony from the second-half of the 12th century to the 16th century, when the disease in Venice eventually declined.

By 1600 the island was abandoned, and remained so until Mechitar, an Armenian monk, fleeing to escape the Ottoman Turks, came to Venice with his community of seventeen monks in 1715. The Venetian Government gave San Lazzaro to Mechitar, who founded an Armenian order on the island, the Mechitarists. The order built a monastery with beautiful cloisters and a stand-alone bell tower with an onion dome (completed in 1750), restored the crumbling lepers' church, and vastly increased the tiny island's area through land reclamation. In 1789, they founded a printing press to spread their language and culture, and they translated many scientific and literary works into Armenian. The monastery flourished and was recognised as an academy by Napoleon in 1810 when nearly all the monasteries in Venice were abolished.

The monastery has a large collection of books, journals, paintings, artefacts, manuscripts, and so forth, housed in a library, a manuscript room, and two museums, all filled with amazing treasures that are on public display. The entire monastery is now surrounded by beautiful park-like gardens with flowers, cypress trees, olive groves, linden trees, rosebushes, hydrangea, peacocks, and a breathtaking view over the Lagoon. The monks also produce their own supply of fruit and vegetables. Today, you can still see the ground level windows of the Church of San Lazzaro, which allowed the sick to observe Mass from outside. Although renovated several times through the centuries, the church still retains the typical, 14th century, Gothic pointed-arch style.

A dear friend of ours, Rico, was in the printing business and spent his first years with the Armenian monks on the island, working with the old printing presses as well as with all the modern technology that had been added over the years. We were fortunate to see the printing works in progress and admire the ancient paper stock and manuscripts. Years later, Lucia and Rico held their daughter Alice's wedding to their son-in-law Giacomo at the lovely old church on the island. We all took boats from the Lido to the jetty which gave us access to the magnificent gardens and the huge terrace, surrounded by a low wall, that looked straight across the Lagoon to Venice. To say the setting was exquisite would be a complete understatement.

Another friend of ours had a business transporting incredible works of art and special artefacts around Venice. He was called to Saint Lazarus Island to arrange the transport of some ancient manuscripts and books to the main library in Venice. Of course, the responsibility and planning for a project of this nature is enormous because the objects are priceless and totally irreplaceable. First, the weather had to present perfect conditions, then a police escort was arranged to accompany the items safely to their new home. Venice certainly has its challenges and costs in caring for, protecting, and maintaining the enormous volume of incredible historic art and artefacts of which they are the guardians and caretakers.

ord Byron was a great lover of Saint Lazarus Island and formed a strong bond with the monks of San Lazzaro. He spent many years there studying the Armenian language and practising meditation. One of his great pleasures was to row cross the narrow expanse of water to the Lido, which he did regularly, and either head for the pale sand dunes and spectacular beaches or do some riding, since he also stabled his horses there.

Ancient monasteries, such as San Lazzaro, contributed significantly to the spread of culture and civilisation, serving as spiritual retreats and places for the devout to study and work. They accommodated monks and pilgrims leaving for the Holy Land, as well as the poor, the helpless and the sick. Many such monasteries in Venice and elsewhere, were later converted into hospitals.

LAZZARETTO NUOVO AND LAZZARETTO VECCHIO

At the entrance to the Venetian Lagoon is the island of Lazzaretto Nuovo or 'New Lazaret', located behind the island of Sant'Erasmo, not to be confused with the island of Lazzaretto Vecchio or 'Old Lazaret', a small island located just off the Lido on the eastern edge of the Lagoon. With the expansion of trade in the Mediterranean during the Middle Ages and the years that followed, Venice faced the danger of epidemics, and it was forced to find solutions to protect its people, maritime traffic, and commerce. Epidemics could not be eradicated; however, the Lagoon's islands could contain epidemics.

The *lazzaretti* are Venice's oldest quarantine stations, intended to protect the city from plague and disease. Lazzaretto Vecchio, established on one of the Venetian islands in 1423, was Venice's first quarantine and hospital facility, used first for leprosy and then for the bubonic plague. In 1468, a second facility was opened on another island, the Lazzaretto Nuovo. The islands respectively, acquired their names from their facilities. The Black Death arrived in Venice in 1348. Two later waves of bubonic plague also hit the city hard in 1576 and again in 1630. The island of Poveglia became the third site used to quarantine and bury victims of these two plagues. Together, these three islands were the centre of Venice's vast public health system.

In 1576, the number of plague victims was so great that many were housed in ships moored off the islands. The Senate of Venice stepped in and hired plague doctors to treat the infected. They wore a special costume and a mask with a prominent beak-shaped nose stuffed with herbs, straw, and spices, which were meant to protect them from the disease. By the time the outbreaks of plague had died down, a third of Venice's population had died.

In the museums on Lazzaretto Nuovo, you can see images and examples of the horrendous beak-like plague masks, which now appear as part of the costumes at Carnival celebrations. Strange that we are back to wearing masks as a result of the Covid-19 epidemic. Our masks today are not quite as ugly but are intended for the same purpose.

When we visited Lazzaretto Nuovo, the atmosphere was charged; we could sense the history of the place and the horror of the dreadful diseases the patients who were housed there had suffered. The buildings that remain demonstrate the skills of the Italian architects and builders, and the remains of the once beautifully designed gardens can still be seen and enjoyed. Archaeological digs on the island have turned up evidence of human habitation in the Bronze Age, and the island serves as the official depository of the Department of Archaeology, Arts and the Landscape for archaeological materials found in the Venetian Lagoon.

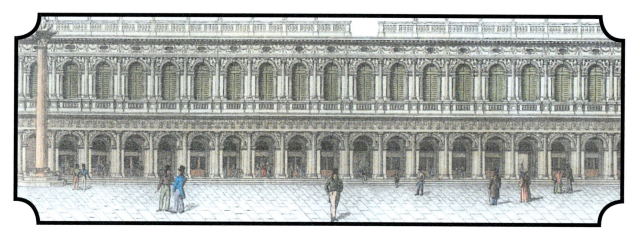

Venice Library

Ducal Palace

8

The Islands of Vignole and Sant'Andrea

VIGNOLE ISLAND

Isola delle *Vignole or* Le *Vignole* – Vignole Island in English – is located north-east of Venice and consists of two islands divided by a canal and connected by a bridge. The entire western island, and the western part of the eastern island, have always been dedicated to horticulture. The rest of the eastern island has always been a military zone, mainly because it faces Venice's principal entrance from the Adriatic Sea. At the eastern island's south-eastern tip, a promontory ends in Sant'Andrea Island, connected to Le Vignole by two bridges. The military zone is quite a contrast to the rest of the island with its landscape covered in market gardens, groves and vineyards.

Le Vignole is a small island of only seventy hectares and is quite rural and sparely inhabited. The few residents, who live in isolated farmstead- type homes and discourage outsiders from wandering about, still make a living mainly from agriculture. They manage with some daily imported labour to tend to what is basically the fruit and vegetable gardens of Venice. With the balance of the land being acres of magnificent vineyards, the grapes grown there have produced the doge's wine since the seventh century.

Today, water vessels of all descriptions take the locals to the island for a day of leisure, produce shopping and eating. In fact, the ancient Romans used the island as a holiday resort. Tables are set out under large shady trees, boats are tied up, great sheets of white paper are spread across the outside dining tables, and the day starts. The island's best and freshest produce of the season is served.

During the afternoons, a steady flow of Venetians turn up to do their weekly shop. They shop not only for themselves but also for their mother, their neighbour, the signora from upstairs, plus any other friends who are in need. It is all quite organised, and while the orders are placed and the bags are being loaded with produce, general gossip and the exchange of information goes on. Every subject may be discussed – from Sunday football and any other football game that may have happened, to the general flow of details about someone's arthritis, or a neighbour who had been taken to hospital, the new baby on the street, and so on. Then the shoppers pick up their bags of goods, pay cash, and off the boats go till next week. I understand that this method of weekly shopping has been going on for hundreds of years.

We would gather a group of friends, obviously boats were required, and then take off for the day and do as described above. We would first have a meal at the restaurant, enjoying the beautiful fresh food and copious amounts of the lovely wine. Over the bridge from the chapel, Chiesa di Santa Maria Assunta e Santa Eurosia alle Vignole, a gateway leads to the Trattoria alle Vignole, a simple restaurant with outdoors space on the shore of the Lagoon and overlooking the Castello district of Venice. We all had our shopping lists and those of our friends. Once we saw to all our purchases, we would load it all on the boat, then head back to Venice or the Lido, where we delivered the goods. We were met with lots of appreciative neighbours, and after sorting out the finance, we took time to have a glass of wine for the trip home, and then away we went. It was very easy to slip into this lifestyle.

The island is a lovely rural place to visit, especially to walk along the paths that meander through the fields. It is not well frequented by tourists as there is not a lot to attract them. In the winter, only the very hardy sea-going individuals among us made the trip across to Le Vignole. The rest of us went out and bought locally.

The chapel, the small Church *of Santa Maria Assunta* and *Santa Eurosia* in *Vignole, has an interesting but tragic tale attached.* The church's 17th century main altar has an altarpiece depicting the Assumption of Saint Mary, and it also has an 18th century painting depicting the Martyrdom of Saint Eurosia, a saint venerated by the island's inhabitants. She is the patron saint of Jaca, a city in north-eastern Spain, in the Pyrenees, and her feast day is 25 June.

Her history is derived from religious writings and there are at least two, fairly different, versions of it. Legend has it that she was of noble birth and was either born in Bayonne, France, in the seventh century, and died in 714; or was born in Bohemia in 864 and died in 880.

In the former version, the more likely of the two, young Eurosia was promised to a Moor in an arranged marriage, but she refused both to marry him and to renounce her Christianity, and she escaped. Eurosia fled into the mountains and hid in a cave where the smoke from her fire led to her capture. She was dragged from the cave by her hair, and her limbs were severed, and then her head removed.

In the latter version, which has very little historical basis but is the most popular, her adoptive father, a duke in Bohemia, was deposed by pagans but then restored to his position by the efforts of Saint Methodius. In 880, Pope John VIII ordered Methodius to bring sixteen-year old Eurosia to Spain, to be married to the son of the king of Pamplona. This prince was heir to the throne of Aragon and Navarre, a powerful ally against the Moors in Spain. Planning to meet her betrothed in Jaca, the bridal party journeyed across the Pyrenees, but the area had become the centre of fierce battles between the Christians and the Saracen warlords. A Moorish captain wanted to marry Eurosia himself and force her to abandon her Christian faith, and he attacked the travellers. Eurosia managed to escape and fled through the mountains, but she was eventually caught. Her hands and feet were amputated and then she was beheaded.

In both versions of the story, her body and its parts were secretly hidden in a cave near the town of Yebra de Basa in the Pyrenees. Many years later, her remains were discovered in the cave by a shepherd. Her head remained at the original site of the discovery, encased in a simple shrine in the Yebra Cavern Hermitage, while her beheaded body was brought to Jaca Cathedral in 935, where it is kept in an urn under the main altar. Various miracles have been attributed to Saint Eurosia.

SANT'ANDREA ISLAND

Several years later, on one of our business trips back to Italy after we had settled in New Zealand, we had a wonderful day trip with our friend Elio to Vignole Island. During our years away from Venice, he had lost his wife, Pierina, to cancer. Fortunately, they had made a trip to New Zealand before she became ill, and we had been able to spend some quality time with her. She was also a remarkably talented artist. On this trip to Vignole Island, he had placed produce orders for, I think, his entire street. In turn, we had placed orders for friends as well. Once the orders were taken, we set off to explore the Lagoon and soon found ourselves at Sant'Andrea Island, the location of the best-preserved fortress on the Lagoon, Forte Sant'Andrea, the Fort of Saint Andrea, which dates back to the 16th century and replaced previously existing defensive works that protected the sea entrance to the Venetian Lagoon. The fort, located close to San Nicolò on the Lido, had always been of strategic importance for the defence of Venice.

At the shore of Sant'Andrea, we pulled our launch alongside a grassy bank on which a big sign was displayed: 'Trespassers will be Prosecuted'. We did as you would expect and tied up! (Italians do not like rules and regulations!) We had just started off through the long grass when we saw the police launch approaching. So there we were, responsible adults, crawling through the grass on our hands and knees. I had dark hair so was told to lay low for fear of being spotted. The guys had light or grey hair, so not as noticeable in the long grass.

The island was overgrown with vegetation and accessible only by private boat. Once we had dodged the cops, we were pretty much the only people there. We could get up off our hands and knees and relax. We made it to the ruins of the ancient fortifications. There we opened a bottle of wine and prepared some food. We made a note of what our reaction would have been had our kids come back from a day trip to the island with the same story!

Once inside the fortress, Renaissance in architectural style, you could only try to imagine how it was built since the entire structure is constructed of small bricks. The builders managed to create beautiful archways, curved windows, and round towers, and to think that all the bricks would have been handmade! The fort presented a military front only on the side facing the inlet of the Lagoon. The other side, facing Venice, was not fortified. It is said this was to ensure the fortress was never used against internal threats, but only to prevent external attacks.

On a lighter note, Venetian Giacomo Casanova (adventurer, author, and by his own account, a great and well-known lover) was detained at the Forte Sant'Andrea from March to July 1743, for his own intrigues. History does not seem to remember exactly what he was in there for, but it was most likely due to owing money. Another clue may lie in the fact that in March 1743, his beloved grandmother died and the Grimanis (his patrons and protectors) enrolled him into San Cipriano Seminary where he was expelled after being found in bed with another boy. Shortly afterwards, he was imprisoned in the Forte Sant'Andrea, probably on the orders of the Grimanis to try to get him back on the straight and narrow. In his memoirs, Casanova wrote an interesting description of the fortress complex and what went on inside. While not used as a prison per se, troublesome people were often put there by the Republic to reconsider their ways.

In 2016, Americans offered to buy the fortress and turn it into a large hotel with all the bells and whistles. Apparently, the city of Venice had already promised to sell it to the private entrepreneurs. Venice's mayor at the time, Luigi Brugnaro, announced that, as part of his plan to "revive the island of Lido", the old Fort of Sant'Andrea would become a luxury development. However, the people of the association Italia Nostra - Venezia, with the assistance of the Venetian Environmental Association (Ambiente Venezia), and the Society for the Protection of Venice, appealed to the Regional Administrative Court of Veneto, and the necessary resolution was not passed, thus the offer was declined.

Daily delivery from Vignole

9

Escape to the Mountain

THE DOLOMITES, JANUARY 1969

Six of us had decided to spend the New Year celebration in the Dolomite Mountains at Franco's brother's hotel in Cortina. As the hotel was fully booked, we were going to have to return to Venice at the end of the evening. This was a pity because the hotel was a delight.

The hotel featured alpine-style architecture, and the plant boxes along the windows and the beautiful wooden balconies were ablaze with red geraniums, vibrant in the cold, crystal-clear sunshine. The restaurant had plate glass windows all around the outside, affording spectacular views of the surrounding mountains. As the sun started to dip, the entire mountain range glowed a bright pink colour. It had to be seen to be believed. Every single patch of snow turned pink, and we spend those few moments outside to experience this wonder. It certainly was something unforgettable.

The central part of the restaurant was cleared for dancing, and it was to be a grand affair. The women had dressed in elegant, full-length evening gowns, mine black with beautiful long sleeves of lace. The men wore their dashing black suits, complete with bow ties. Franco's sister Elda had designated a small box room where we could change into our evening wear. While a long, formal evening gown was appropriate and expected, it was not sufficiently warm, but thanks to my magic fur coat, I could dress up in a beautiful gown in the winter.

The food arrived, one delicious course after the other. The Italians do know their food. We had platters of fish, antipasto, cheeses, cold meats and salads as our entrée. You expect amazing fish in Venice, but not in the mountains, yet they had a vast range to offer, all perfectly fresh and exquisitely prepared. The pasta course followed, the star dish being an amazing mushroom risotto. Mushrooms, of course, being another food that is prolific in the mountains, and not to be missed either, are the renowned truffles of the region. On the properties you passed by in that part of the country, you could always see the pigs that were being raised to find the truffles in the woods. The main course was a selection of all the meats, vegetables and salads possible. Thank heavens we were dancing that evening, or it would have been quite a challenge to get moving.

This region of Trentino is famous for its Prosecco, the product of the amazing white grapes that grow almost wild in the area. It is Italy's answer to French champagne. We looked at importing it into New Zealand ourselves once we had settled here, but then chose instead to deal in Italian designer lighting. Thank goodness, however, this amazing product is now well established in New Zealand.

The New Year Eve's celebration was great and the meal incredible. We saw in the new year then took action to get back down the mountain safely. It must have been thirty below and the cars' engines wouldn't start. We had to push-start the cars into life, and at first there wasn't much flat road for the men to run and push the cars along, not to mention the ice on the road. Eventually, though, we took off down the very narrow, windy road in what seemed like a total blackout. No streetlights, no traffic, no moon. It was horrendous.

We finally arrived in Venice. Of course the car ferry had left, and we had to park the cars at a designated parking site in Piazzale Roma, where there were no water taxis available at that hour, so we had a very long walk from one end of Venice to the other. Fortunately, at another stop in Venice we did manage to get a water taxi to take us across to the Lido, a trip of about ten to fifteen minutes, followed by a long walk home. I think it was close to four in the morning when we got in. This reinforced the need to make detailed plans when you lived in Venice. There were so many elements to take into consideration.

I was now developing a friendship with a lovely group of international young women who spoke English. We were able to exchange English language books and news from home, wherever that was for each of us. We could also discuss our ongoing dilemmas with the language, the way of life, the husbands, and so on. On one occasion I was visiting Elaine, who was from the UK, in her home on the Lido, an old villa facing the Venetian Lagoon. We were chatting away when a contractor knocked on the door and in the usual flamboyant Italian way, said, "Sorry to disturb you. Would you object if I walked across your roof to install cables to next-door's house?" The word 'roof ' in Italian is 'tetto'.

In very elegant but flawed Italian, Elaine replied, "At your leisure, you may walk across our tits." She used the word 'titi' in Italian. When the pink-faced contractor left, we fell about laughing at ourselves and the *risqué* error. Later, when we reported the story to the husbands, strangely, they did not find it quite as hilarious as we had!

VAJONT, FEBRUARY 1969

Shortly after the New Year Eve's party in the mountains and well before the end of the winter, we were invited to a friend's wedding. Lucia and Rico had been friends for a very long time, ever since he came to Lido to join the Lido soccer team. Lucia had grown up on the Lido and had spent all her life there. In fact, Franco used to play with her two older brothers as a child, and he had known Lucia since she was a baby. We were spending a lot of time with them, and to this day I can only thank Lucia for my command of the Italian language. I recall walking for kilometres along the beach while trying to communicate with her in Italian. She always gently corrected me when the local dialect fell out of my mouth; she felt I should learn Italian first, and the regional dialect second. Her patience was quite something. Trying to describe a tortoiseshell comb I had purchased, I told her that it was "a little animal that carries his house on his back" and it took quite a while for her to understand what I meant!

The wedding was lovely, and we waved them off on their trip to the house they had booked in the Dolomite Mountains. About two weeks later they rang to ask if we would drive up and join them on their honeymoon, along with another couple, Aldo and Stefania, also from Venice. We found it rather strange to be invited to spend their honeymoon with the newlywed couple! After numerous phone calls, it was agreed we would all go, but not for very long though.

The house they had rented was very rustic and built of wood in a typical Austrian-alpine design. It was small and basic, and the bathroom essentially consisted of a pipe with a nozzle, this being the shower, and the toilet was outside. The house was certainly not even one-star accommodation, but it was set in what could only be described as a wonderland of nature. The beautiful mountains, the forests, the clear blue sky, and so isolated.

The two bedrooms were small and sleeping arrangements became an issue. I was in a double bed with Aldo and Stefania, and Franco in a single bed, all in one of the bedrooms. The married couple were in the second bedroom, in a double bed. It was then decided Franco and I should get into bed with Lucia and Rico. The debate about the suitability of this went on for a very long time. Of course, we did not think it was a friendly deal to make with a honeymoon couple. We lost, they insisted we share their bed, and we talked and laughed all night.

The milk we used was from a local farmer's cow, and cooking was done on an old, black, wood-burning iron stove. We could have been living in the year 1915. Lucia had the situation well in hand, though. Being a great cook, she had things cooking along in no time. Fortunately, we had all taken up enough food to feed an army. There was also an ample supply of Clinto, the local mountain wine, quite rough with a unique taste: intense, acid and raw. It has a distinct perfume and a very dark red colour, almost violet, that stains everything. I doubt our systems would be so agreeable today.

After a day out in the snow and climbing up and down the valleys, we came home to a big, welcoming fire, and put some food on the table. Franco had his guitar, so we sang the old, traditional mountain ballads, drank the rough red Clinto, and slept like babies.

We do have a delightful photo of Franco taken on that trip. He had gone out to collect the milk and had thrown on Lucia's dressing gown. The results of the previous evening's Clinto session ensured that he did not make a pretty sight.

On the way back to Venice, we drove by Vajont Dam, one of the tallest dams ever built, with a height of 262 metres, and one of the world's biggest dams at the time of its completion in 1959. It is situated in the valley of the Vajont River under Monte Toc, a hundred kilometres north of Venice, and is no longer in use. On the night of 9 October 1963, during the initial filling, 260 million cubic metres of rock broke off from the top of Monte Toc. It fell into the dam's reservoir, producing an enormous wave of at least 50 million cubic metres of water that rose more than 250 metres above the dam before plunging headlong towards the village of Longarone, directly in its path in the valley of the River Piave. The inland tsunami, travelling at 100 kilometres per hour and pushing an air pocket ahead of it, struck with tremendous force, leading to the complete destruction of several villages and towns. An estimated 1,900 to 2,500 people died, most of the bodies never recovered. The dam itself did not collapse or suffer any serious damage, which was a credit to its design and engineering. Still, it was built in the wrong place with too little attention paid to geological reports, potential tectonic problems, local knowledge of the area, and Monte Toc's instability. Frankly, even as the dam was being built, the fear that Monte Toc would collapse was widespread in the area. The people in this region were very dour and hard-working and time seemed to have stood still for them; they appeared to be living twenty years behind the cities. We had a problem communicating with them, and our worse dilemma was when Franco was asked to buy a supply of condoms from the local shop, the only one in the village. The next thing we saw was Franco running up the hill, being chased by an old man with a broom, shouting and calling him a dirty boy! Franco was shouting back, "I am twenty-seven and married!"

We all promised to be very nice to Franco from then on. More than forty years later, we still can't help but leave the room (in fits of giggles) when that holiday is brought up.

The Dolomite Mountain Range

New Year's Eve party

10

The Arsenal

Although it is of historical importance, Arsenale di Venezia, the Arsenal of Venice, located on Castello Island, is a place that usually escapes the horde of tourists. For centuries, though, the massive armoury and shipyard was the heart and strength of the naval industry of Venice and its islands. Today, part of the historic *Arsenal* still serves as a naval base and does not permit visitors, but a large section is open to the public, and a naval museum is located in the building of the former granary. The scale of the architecture and the industrial history of the Arsenal is impressive. Construction of the Arsenal began around 1104 on the order of the Doge of Venice, Ordelafo Faliero, and it served as the Venetian military headquarters for centuries afterwards. In the 14th century the construction was completed and expanded, and in the 15th and 16th centuries, it was rebuilt again. By 1500 it was, until the 18th century, Europe's largest industrial complex, comprising a vast cluster of basins, shipyards, and workshops for making sails, ropes and ordnance.

While the building is mainly of a Byzantine style, its main entrance, the Porta Magna, created in 1460 by the famous architect of that time, Bellini, features an elaborately decorated gateway in a Renaissance style. It is guarded by two huge stone lions.

It initially spanned an area of 8 acres, later expanded to 110 acres, which was about fifteen per cent of the land mass of Venice at the time. It was enclosed by a rampart 3.2 metres in height, and high walls hid the interior secrets from the public. Nowadays, its spacious halls, landscaped gardens, and beautiful lawns overlooking the harbour, are used as one of the main venues for La Biennale di Venezia, one of the world's most prestigious cultural institutions, established in 1895.

The Arsenal built most of Venice's maritime trading vessels, as well as military vessels, and created an enormous economy that enabled Venice to fund the design and construction of the magnificent city we see today. This lasted until the fall of the Venetian Republic to Napoleon in 1797. The Arsenal had a tightly organised shipyard that employed highly efficient production methods, including the first assembly lines, the use of standardised parts, quality control, and a specialised workforce, to mention but a few innovations. The Arsenal also developed a just-in- time, prefabricated production system, with different areas focusing on a particular part of the ship or specific piece of maritime equipment, such as munitions rope, oars and rigging. This not only increased efficiency but also limited any one worker learning too many valuable manufacturing secrets.

The shipyard could produce one to two ships a day. It was how the famous galleys were built that allowed Venice to control the most important maritime routes of the Mediterranean. The Arsenal also owned large forests in the Montello area of the Lombardy Region of Italy, west of Venice, which provided all the wood required for the massive enterprise In 1593, Galileo became a consultant at the Arsenal, helping to solve many of the shipbuilders' problems and advising military engineers and instrument makers on ballistics, production and logistics. His book *Discourses and Mathematical Demonstrations Concerning Two New Sciences* (1638), which addressed the new field of modern sciences dealing with the strength and resistance of materials and the study of military armoury and munitions, was of great assistance to the Venetian shipbuilders.

The *arsenalotti,* those employed by the Arsenal, worked up to eleven hours per day in summer and six in winter. The young people who did the really hard work did not have much in terms of quality of life. They started off at the Arsenal as very young boys, trying to help with the family food bills. They were given one job and it could last a lifetime. As mentioned, they were specialised and segregated into work areas, each separate from the other to avoid the transfer of information. Special entrances and access ways were in place to ensure complete isolation between work areas. Unions had not yet been established, although there were guilds in place. Any small transgression and you could be shot on the spot.

There were some advantages for the workers though. Besides being more or less guaranteed lifetime employment, they also benefited from Europe's first pension system. Another bonus was that certain workers qualified for family housing. Located just outside of the walls of the Arsenal, streets of small, attached cottages served as the workers' homes. If a worker had been with the company for close to a lifetime, he could get a cottage. Once the old man died, the cottage could stay in the family if there was a son to continue his work at the Arsenal. Daughters did not count in this respect. While women were also employed, mainly to cut, sew and repair canvas in the enormous sail lofts, they could not access housing benefits. The cottages are still there today. I think the first doll's house we had made for our girls to play in was larger than any of those cottages.

Although rare, Venice has been subjected to tornados, the most recent being in 2012, 2015 and 2016. On 11 September 1970, a tornado, *tromba d'aria* (trumpet of the air) in Italian, ripped through Castello, the area where the Arsenal is located, and destroyed many roofs along a very narrow path it cut toward the edge of the Lagoon. There it picked up a motorscafo, which, being the local means of transport, is always full of passengers, so much so that you expect to stand all the way to your destination. To estimate the full weight of the vessel plus passengers would be difficult, but on this terrible day the motoscafo, complete with all the passengers, was lifted out of the water by the tornado, turned upside down and slammed back down again, killing at least twenty-one people. The same weather system, on the same day, saw one or more tornadoes unleashed through the wider Venetian region, killing as many as fifty people, including those who lost their lives in the motoscafo.

Arsenal

11

An Addition to the Family

JESSICA IS BORN. SPRING, APRIL 1971

During the summer months of 1970, I found I was expecting our first child. I was confident with my Italian, but thought, *Here we go again with an entirely new vocabulary to master.* My sister-in-law Lilly became the general- in-chief as Franco was obviously as green as I was. We went round and round with my antenatal care – blood tests, weighing in, nutritional plans, and so on. I would hunt down one of the many English-speaking girlfriends I had acquired to help me work my way through this challenge. I was feeling very homesick at this time, and earlier, in 1969, Franco had applied to Alitalia, the Italian airlines, for a position. It was not easy as applicants had to speak three languages, which he did, but he still had to spend two months topping up his qualifications. He had to go to Verona to sit exams, and whilst there, the breaking news of the first landing of humans on the Moon was on television.

Jessica was born in April 1971, at the Ospedale al Mare, the Hospital of the Sea, on the island of Lido. The hospital was literally on the beach and surrounded by beautiful gardens. Established in 1868, it was once used mainly as a centre for the treatment of tuberculosis. It developed into a healthcare facility offering alternative treatments, such as heliotherapy, hydrotherapy, beaches, and opera!

In 2003, the hospital was closed down and became abandoned. The property has changed hands a few times over the years and plans or promises have been made more than once to restore, renovate or redevelop the hospital's sprawling complex of buildings, which included an old theatre (Teatro Marinoni, later known as Il Teatrino Liberty), a church, a library, workshops for artisans, multiple kitchens, full laundry facilities, a school, and shops. But as of 2017, the dilapidated property became the haunt of graffiti artists and squatters. Even today, despite numerous bidders for the property, it remains derelict, and unless a wealthy benefactor or developer steps forward, it will most likely be demolished. While at the hospital, I met a lovely student nurse, Ruzena, from Czechoslovakia, as it was then called. She had to give me an injection, and it was the first time she would be injecting a patient. She was studying nursing by translating from Czech to English, and then from English to Italian, using dictionaries for each language. And doing the reverse when it came to the course material. We became very close friends; her husband was yet another of Franco's buddies.

All went well with Jessica's birth, and she came home with two very inexperienced parents, but an entire world on standby to help. Italians love babies. The women talk about their childbirth experiences in a wonderful open way, some of which I found a little disconcerting having a very British background. Even the guys would get involved with the details, friends would see me out and about and ask for a step-by-step account of the labour I endured, even wanting intimate details, such as whether stitches were required, and so forth.

We inherited one of those huge old-fashioned English prams, with the big wheels and sprung chassis, from my sister-in-law, which was an excellent choice for life on the Lido, seeing as how much walking we did. At the time there had been talk about baby snatching going on in Rome and in the South, so a shopping trip with Jessica in the pram was a bit of a mission. Because the shops were too small to accommodate the pram, or even to get it in through the entrance, I would have to stand outside and shout out my shopping list from the door. I was not going to turn my back on that pram. The usual wonderful care I received from the Venetians came into play. When it was my turn to call out from the door, the shop assistant would ask everyone to shut up so *la signora Inglese*, the English lady, could place her order. The next thing I noticed was that someone would invariably stop and say they would stand by the pram while I did my shopping. Once, a friend of Franco's was rushing home from work but stopped and said he could hang with the baby while I got the shopping done! I found this real care and interest so very touching, and he and I walked home together, pushing the pram.

While getting on the boats with the large pram, another unwritten law was in place. On the Lido, as you approached the vessel, the boatmen would just simply bend down and lift the pram aboard. Likewise in the main city of Venice with all those bridges and their stone stairs, a random guy would, unbidden, just lift the front of the pram and get me across to the other side. Another time, when the baby was a little unsettled, one of Franco's friends said he would wheel Jessica up and down the street while I did my shopping. Not to mention the hours I spent replying to those who asked after her: Was she eating well? How was she at night? Have I tried this biscuit or that? Many of these people were strangers or people I barely knew. The level of interest in her well-being was quite lovely.

My group of foreign girlfriends and I would all meet at the park and swap books, information, medical advice, and so forth. There was an entire new world out there and more advice to be had than in the *Encyclopaedia Britannica*. We survived beautifully. We had a lovely paediatrician who came to the apartment to see Jessica for her regular check-ups, and who continued to provide all the care any baby and mother could ask for. At one stage, I was about to undress Jessica for her usual examination, but the doctor said, "Don't bother. Look at her! We would be hard-pressed to find a more healthy-looking baby." This was a huge step forward for me and most encouraging as I had questioned myself as to Jessica's chance of survival with a mother who had never handled a baby before!

12

A New Home

We were told an apartment in our block was going to be available to rent in a couple of months. Accommodation on Lido Island was, and remains, a significant issue. There were no real estate offices because any accommodation that became vacant was filled within a few days via word of mouth. Apparently, this is still largely the case. Franco and our small family had been living in an internal (inward-facing) apartment in a block of four buildings. Now a ground-floor, external-facing apartment had become available. It had two bedrooms and was a real delight. We were fortunate to secure the lease. Our balcony now looked out over a picturesque canal lined with big trees on one side and elegant gated-villas on the other. The canal curved slightly to the left toward the basin of the Palazzo del Casinò, the Venice Casino. This basin is where the punters arrived by boat and entered the casino on a plush red carpet to get to the gaming rooms. I have heard that a body was once found in our canal, a sorry gambler who must have lost the lot. Fortunately, this was not a regular occurrence.

The imposing Palazzo del Casinò, designed by Eugenio Miozzi in the Rationalist style, was built in the record time of eight months in 1938. Despite its austere facade, the interior was sumptuous and remains so. The magnificent staircase, marble floors and columns, ceiling mosaics, Murano glass, and chandeliers are worth seeing. In the late 1990s, the Casinò was closed in terms of gambling, and the Palazzo is now used for other purposes, such as the Venice Biennale, conventions and exhibitions, and the Venice International Film Festival. Close by is the Palazzo del Cinema, inaugurated in 1937 and in the Rationalist style too, which is the main venue for the Venice International Film Festival.

The convenience with these lovely new apartments on the Lido, such as the one in which we lived, was that firstly, on the ground floor there was accommodation for the caretakers (a husband and wife) who were always on hand if you needed anything. And secondly, that a storage room on the ground floor was allocated to each tenant. Ours held prams, pushchairs, bikes, et cetera, which meant I had to carry only the baby to the first floor. La Signora was always on hand to help me by bringing up the shopping, or the baby, or just to be of assistance and keep me informed on the general goings-on in the area!

We were infrequent visitors to the Casinò but did see some wonderful films there during the film festivals. The rich and famous, with their huge entourages, arrived to this very glamorous event to be gawked at by spectators. Yes, even in Italy, elegant and famous people walking around or being collected by incredibly huge American cars, was something that got noticed. The lights, music, and dancing in the piazza in front of the red-carpeted buildings during the Venice Film Festival made life very busy for us.

Since we had a baby, we decided to share the load with our dearest friends, Lucia and Rico, who had not started their family yet. One night during a film festival, the boys went to see a film while we girls babysat Jessica. The next night the girls went to the movies and the boys stayed home. When we all sat down to discuss the film Lucia and I had seen, which was a very steamy, partially nude sort of film, it turned out that the lady who had been on screen without any clothes on, had been seated just in front of us. The boys had seen a film very much to do with the Church – monks, friars, and nuns. No one, however, had taken their clothes off! We found this very entertaining. Thereafter though, similar excursions were well researched beforehand.

Just across from the Piazza Della Cinema on the Lido is the Excelsior Hotel, dating from 1908. It was inaugurated with a lavish beach party for more than three thousand invited guests from around the world. Thirty thousand Venetian residents came to observe the event. It is still one of Venice's most iconic luxury hotels. Its exterior design is very much that of a Venetian Renaissance palace, complete with a golden, onion-domed tower. The hotel's interior is a blend of Belle Époque architecture and Moorish design touches. More than a century since its dramatic opening, the exclusive hotel is still popular among those seeking opulence and a level of service rarely seen since the Golden Age. It was the inspiration of the great architect Giovani Sardi and the entrepreneur Nicola Spada, who transformed the Lido Venice into a sought-after destinations for the wealthy and glamorous. Some of the distinguished guests in the past include Winston Churchill, the Duke and Duchess of Windsor, Marlene Dietrich, Barbara Hutton, John Steinbeck, Ingrid Bergman, the Aga Khan, minor royalty, and the aristocracy. Today, of course, the list is much longer and no less impressive.

We had a few occasions to pop into the Hotel Excelsior for a drink. To have a meal there, however, would have cost us a month's salary, so living within minutes of the place certainly gave Franco a good excuse to make his escape before I so much as thought, or suggested, that it would be nice to stay for dinner.

The long driveway that ran from our apartment building down to the street, passed along beside the tennis courts of the Albergo Quattro Fontane, the Four Fountains Hotel. The hotel's name recalls the four large underground cisterns, existing since the Roman Era and reactivated by the Serenissima Republic, where the rainwater filtered by the dunes was once collected to supply the town and the various fortifications of the Lido with fresh water. At a time when European cities depended on rivers, spring-fed aqueducts, and groundwater wells as their sources of fresh water, Venice exploited a fourth option: a complex network of cisterns for capturing, filtering and storing rainwater. When coming across what are generally referred to as 'wells' in Venice, it is worth noting that they are in fact not wells at all, but underground cisterns. Wells would merely tap into brackish or even polluted groundwater.

Our biggest problem in the area where we lived was parking our little Fiat 850 on the street reasonably close to our apartment during the summer season. A lot of the nearby cars were Porches, Ferraris, Lamborghinis and Jaguars, belonging to or leased by the wealthy staying in their holiday accommodations. Soon we overcame this problem by purchasing a smashing little scooter for our summer transport.

13

The Scooter

In the spring Franco purchased a scooter, which was ideal on the small island of Lido. There were no car park buildings, then or now, but a lot of families still had two cars, as we eventually did too. The bus–boat system of public transport on Lido, though, was fantastic. As you got off the boat, the bus was waiting for the next leg of your trip, and the reverse. The distance from the bus stop to any home on the island could not have been more than a ten-minute walk. We parked our car for the summer and followed the hundreds of scooters travelling the island. The fun was that you could stop anywhere and talk to anyone!

One of the first expeditions on scooter was when Franco decided to make an aquarium for Jessica. He had built the structure's top and base, and now needed the panes for the sides. To get the glass home from the shop by scooter meant that he had to have one knee sticking out rigidly to support the panes. This modest means of transport could carry anything if you put your mind to it. We spent many happy days going fishing, with the scooter loaded with long rods, a picnic basket, swimming gear, and whatnot. No helmets required either.

Once Jessica started kindergarten, Franco would often drop her off on the scooter on the way to work. In the winter, she wore a heavy coat, a hat and gloves to protect her from the elements. Franco, always running late, would go out with wet hair. I voiced my opinion about head colds and so on. He felt a trip on the scooter in the brisk weather was the best way to dry your hair!

The beauty of the scooter was that as you drove by, you would see friends walking along or on their scooters, and then conveniently stop to chat. Consequently, using a scooter meant that getting from A to B could take a very long time and it had nothing to do with traffic. There was a special place along most streets where we could park and the children could play while we put the world to rights, then on our way we went again.

Another great summer experience on the Lido were the rooftop parties. If you had a top-floor apartment and you were friendly with your neighbours below, you could throw a party, which happened quite often. Food and drinks were carried up to the roof and music set up through a window or by means of an extension lead, and the party began.

Our friends had a top-floor apartment facing the Lagoon, with the city of Venice as a backdrop. As the sun set over Venice on a clear day, the view of the Dolomite Mountains visible behind the skyline of the city could only be described as magical. As the evening progressed, the city lights slowly came on and Venice took on a cloak of mystery. We would talk and dance and party and yes, of course, sort out the Italian Government.

14

A Trip to Paris

_____

In the spring, Paris traditionally hosts the Spring Fashion Week, where top designers show their fashions for the year ahead. Franco had been involved in getting groups of fashion houses and designers on flights to the event. The outcome, and I am not quite sure why we deserved this, was that we were given tickets on the same flight. As we had three-year-old Jessica, we took her along too. We had one of the first models of those little foldaway pushchairs that we could take on the plane. We were very cautious as we were quite new to international travel with a child in tow! The flight went well with no significant child-related incidents.

Our hotel was on the Avenue des Champs-Élysées, absolute five-star and not many little ones running around! The interior was classic Louie XIV in style: plush red and gold, elegantly carved gilded chairs, furniture inlaid with plaques of copper and exotic woods, divine fabrics for the drapery, and so on. We had two bedrooms and a beautiful view of the most elegant street in Paris, and yes, it was well beyond our budget! The Alitalia staff discount privileges made it possible.

We dropped our bags and took off for a walk, and that is what we did for three days. Jessica was so good; she just seemed to have become an expert people-watcher! We purchased food from the deli, the *traiteur* or *épicerie fine* – ham, cheese, olives and bread – as we knew we could not keep her up for late dinner at the hotel. There was also the cost factor to consider! We were very careful to pick up crumbs off the floor and removed all evidence that we had eaten in the room. As the years went by, we realised that babysitters are always available at such upmarket hotels, and we could have gone out on the town, but that was to come later. We loved every step we walked in Paris, the photos we took, and the places of historical and cultural significance we saw. Simply being there was enough for us. We visited Montmartre and Sacré-Coeur Basilica, the Eiffel Tower, and the Left Bank.

We went to the Louvre Museum to see Leonardo da Vinci's *Mona Lisa.* There we learnt of the Italian, Vincenzo Peruggia, a former worker at the Louvre, who stole the famous artwork in 1911. The French Police believe that on the night of Sunday 20 August, he hid inside the museum knowing it would be closed the following day. But Peruggia said that he simply walked into the museum on the Monday morning through a door that the other Louvre workers were entering. Since he wore one of the white smocks that the workers customarily wore, no one noticed him. Once the hall in which the *Mona Lisa* hung was empty, he took the painting to a service staircase where he removed its protective case and frame. He said he took off his smock and wrapped it around the painting, tucked it under his arm, and left the Louvre through the same door he had entered. At first, he hid the painting in a trunk in his apartment in Paris for two years. Then he returned to Italy with it and kept it in his apartment in Florence for some time. Peruggia grew impatient and contacted the owner of an art gallery. It transpired that he expected a reward for returning the painting to Italy, its 'homeland'. Needless to say, Peruggia was soon arrested, and the painting returned to the Louvre in 1913.

When we visited, neither the Louvre Pyramid, constructed of glass and metal (completed in 1988), situated in the Napoleon Courtyard, nor the Louvre Inverted Pyramid, a skylight (completed in 1993), located in the middle of the roundabout of the Place du Carrousel, had been built yet. Both were designed by I. M. Pei.

It is said that Mary Magdalene is buried below the floor of the Museum, beneath the hidden portion of a tiny stone pyramid visible above the floor, which almost touches the tip of the inverted glass pyramid. This, however, has not been confirmed. Jessica developed a real passion for art history, and we like to believe this trip to Paris lit the spark.

When we boarded the flight back to Venice, our travel companions were going on about the money they had spent on taxis and how exhausted they were. We had walked the entire area and barely used a taxi, so had saved a bit of money, and Franco ordered champagne on the way home. We felt we had done well. Our first venture as travellers with a child in tow was declared a success. We knew we had to make this call if we wanted to travel. We decided that when Franco travelled, the family would come too! Not long after our return from Paris, we started to prepare for the Annual Alitalia Employee Picnic. We had the opportunity to enter several competitions – photography, storytelling, artwork, poetry, or stand-up comedy (the jokes had to be clean). On the day of the picnic, the entries would be judged, and the winners announced. Franco entered a photo of Jessica all fitted out in scuba-diving gear. It was not easy to tie it all together, but she did look very cute. The standard of the competition was quite something, very impressive. The Italians actively encourage the arts among their people, starting at a very young age. From the time children first go to school, they all have a Memory Book, in which they and their friends draw pictures, or write little stories, or add comments, and the children all start off with a new one each year. This tradition certainly gave us parents a lovely picture and memento of our child's development and friendships.

The day of the picnic continued with sporting events. Father and child three-legged races, the father racing with his lower leg tied to that of his child, for instance. Women's races were held too, and since we mothers took turns sharing the supervision of our children, we could all participate. The lunchtime meal was in a large, open garden under the grapevines. The older children took turns to look after the little ones while the adults carried on with conversations that went on for hours.

Street in Venice

15

La Fenice

SEPTEMBER 1972

I had grown up in a home filled with opera music, my mother's passion. I remember doing a lot of washing up to the sound of operas. Each time my brother was told to help with the task, we had fights about two things to get the job done: first, that he should work a bit faster to dry the dishes, and second, that I splashed water at him when he turned the volume of the opera music down! For Franco, being Italian, he had grown up with opera and knew more about it than I ever had.

La fenice, the phoenix, associated with classical mythology, is an immortal bird whose origin is considered to be in Egypt. It is believed that the phoenix lived for five centuries in the Arabian Desert, at the end of which it burned itself on a funeral pyre and then rose again from the ashes, reborn to live through another cycle of life and renewal. Sadly, this is a well-chosen name for Teatro La Fenice, La Fenice Opera House, situated in the heart of Venice, only five minutes from Piazza San Marco. In 1774, the Teatro San Benedetto, which had been Venice's leading opera house for more than forty years, burned to the ground. By 1789, a number of wealthy opera lovers expressed an interest in funding and building a spectacular new opera house to replace Teatro San Benedetto, and they launched a competition to find a suitable architect and design. Giannantonio Selva was the winner. Construction began in June 1790, and the theatre, named Teatro La Fenice, was inaugurated on 16 May 1792. It was destroyed by fire twice since then and was rebuilt each time.

The first fire was in December 1836, and the theatre company decided to go ahead with its reconstruction immediately. On 26 December 1837, just like the mythical phoenix, La Fenice rose again in even greater beauty and splendour. The second fire was on 29 January 1996, when flames destroyed the five tiers of boxes, the stage, and the ceiling. Only the perimeter walls of the original structure remained. Arson was immediately suspected and in March 2001, a court in Venice found two disgruntled electricians guilty of the crime. Reconstruction of the building began in 2001 and La Fenice reopened in 2003, beautifully restored to its former glory, the craftmanship so immaculate that not a trace remained of the damage. The instruction given to the architect Aldo Rossi was to rebuild it *"com'era, dov'era"* – "as it was, where it was". Its exquisite rococo decor, complete with glittering gold leaf and magnificent chandeliers, makes this an ideal venue for opera, classical ballet, symphony and theatre performances.

The Giacomelli family had the first box on the right, just above the stage. Given its grandeur, it is so hard to grasp that after the devastation of the fires, its present form and appearance are not the original. The deep-pink plush fabric on all the seats is rewoven pure silk, prepared and stitched as per the old method. The gilded decorations are all of old gold-leaf and applied with techniques practised by artisans over hundreds of years.

We were fortunate to have a friend who had access to behind the scenes at La Fenice, and he took us on a tour. The piano that Verdi always practised on was there. The wardrobes of costumes and dresses were all back in place, and fortunately, most of the ancient music scores and manuscripts had been restored. It took almost eight years from the fire in 1996, to rebuild the theatre, wardrobes and music archives.

We have had many very special evenings in this real gem of Venice. On one occasion, just prior to going to the opera, I had already put my coat on but then had to run upstairs to bring in the washing. It had all dried beautifully on the roof of the apartment block. I quickly folded the laundry and rushed to get Jessica to bed. Rico and Lucia were babysitting for us. Finally, I was seated in the box at La Fenice, gazing down at the incredible sight of its sumptuous interior – the gold, the splendour, all quite magical. As I took my coat off, I found a handful of washing pegs still in my pocket! *Just a little reality check to keep me grounded*, I thought.

Our close friends Elio and Pierina have a very talented daughter, Caterina, who, along with her husband, Zokol, also a great musician, play regularly at La Fenice Opera House when they are not on tour around Europe. We had so many beautiful experiences in that theatre, and I will never forget the magic as the lights dim and the curtain goes up.

We were invited to the spectacular wedding of these two talented musicians. It was held on the rooftop of a very old building close to Arsenale di Venezia, the Arsenal. We dined downstairs in the garden, but the after-party was upstairs on the roof garden. From this vantage point, we could look across the Lagoon to all the other Venetian Islands. To say Venice had turned on her splendour yet again that night, does not really do justice to the spectacular sights and events that can be seen and experienced there.

Many years later, I took my granddaughter Heidi from New Zealand on a trip to Venice and to La Fenice Opera House; she was only fourteen years old at the time. To see her eyes light up, told me La Fenice had not lost her magic despite some troubled times in her history.

16

A Holiday in New Zealand

In July 1974, we booked a trip to New Zealand to introduce Franco and Jessica to the rest of the family whom they had not met. I was also four months pregnant with our second baby, so the window of opportunity for long-haul travel was restricted.

We flew via Athens to Bombay and then Sydney, and finally, landed in Auckland. Our concern was that Jessica, only a little older than three and who understood English very well, would reply in Italian with the odd English word thrown in for good measure. As we approached the barrier at the Arrivals concourse in Auckland, my father was waving, and somehow recognising him as family, Jessica simply put her arms up and went straight to him. Needless to say, this was the start of a lovely bond. He tried to learn Italian, but instead, Jessica found she was better at English, having forged ahead rapidly with the language.

New Zealand was, and remains, very different to Europe. At the time, there were approximately four million people in New Zealand, while Italy had a population of sixty-four million. The land area of Italy, excluding Sardinia, is about the same as that of New Zealand. This paucity of population means that in New Zealand we have kilometre upon kilometre of white sandy beaches, deserted islands, wild tropical bush, and thick forests. To go on a day out, you need to take everything with you – there are no bars, no waiters, no tukuls, no shops, and no facilities once you are away from the cities and towns. Introducing my Italian husband to this way of living was going to prove a problem. To start with, our sunshine is so incredibly intense in summer that sunburn was issue number one. Then along came the sandflies, tiny little things that bite like hell and leave you scratching for days. Our coastal waters, unlike the beautiful, calm waters of Lido Venice's Adriatic, are wild, cold, and very powerful. At the beach in New Zealand we climbed rocks and picked huge oysters. Franco could not believe the size of them. Getting him to eat the oysters without a touch of lemon was another issue! The oysters from the Adriatic, which he was accustomed to, are so small, but very delicate and tasty.

My brother and family have a beautiful beach house on the North Island's Coromandel Peninsular, which is along the east coast. From there you look straight across the Pacific Ocean towards South America. One day my brother rang for advice on cooking squid. Franco's advice was to simply boil a pot of water and then just put the squid in. Malcolm rang back two hours later to say the squid was still tough.

The squid available in Venice are tiny, dainty little things. Malcolm's squid was nearly four kilograms in weight! When my bother saw Franco's fishing rods, he thought they would be quite good for knitting!

We went down to stay with my brother and sister-in-law for a short break. Malcolm had an outboard which he used for fishing. Snapper was on the menu, so husband, brother and brother-in-law went out on the water to catch snapper for the barbeque. As the boat approached the jetty, a huge swell picked it up and turned it over. No one was hurt and the family thought it was the funniest thing that had happened that year, while Franco sat silent, in a state of shock.

Poor Franco. By the time we returned home to Venice, he had been attacked by everything that could bite or sting, was sunburnt, had been battered on the rocks, been chased by bulls on a friend's farm, and been covered in muck from a milking shed. Also, he wondered what sort of a mad family he had married into!

I could almost feel his sigh of relief as he got back into his designer gear, and we headed for Venice, for home.

17

Nathalie is Born

On 25 December 1974, Nathalie was born. Besides our small family, all the doctors and nurses also missed Christmas Day. I was only four hours in labour; at the speed she was going, she could have landed on the beach in front of the hospital! Her father, her aunt, and the medical team all looked stunned. They decided that Kiwi mothers are just inherently tough. We came home to our lovely doctor and her regular house visits that continued until it looked as though Nathalie was in good hands and not under threat by having an inexperienced mother.

We all decided that Franco was determined to have his children born on special days. Jessica was born on 25 April, which is St Mark's Day, St Mark being the patron saint of Venice. On this day, all the men give the special women in their lives – their mother, daughter, wife – one red rose. The city becomes a massive display of colour and smiles as all the women have a red rose in hand. It is also Anzac Day in New Zealand, commemorating the New Zealanders killed in war, especially those who fell at Anzac Cove on the Gallipoli Peninsula, Turkey, in 1915, and it honours returned and serving servicemen and -women. I think Franco had a thing about festive occasions. If we had tried for a boy, I am sure he would have been born on Easter Sunday.

Nathalie was an easy baby, and we soon had a routine. However, as they say – one is one and two are twenty-two, and I was busy. It was a cold winter, so going out with an infant was not an option for a good many days. Fortunately, Jessica had started kindergarten, so Nathalie escaped her continuous caring attention and got some sleep! I think Jessica really did think Santa Claus or Babbo Natale had brought her a baby to play with as a gift. I do remember on one occasion, later in July when we were sweltering under forty degree heat, I had pulled out clothes from some cupboards to pack away downstairs in our storage room. The girls' room was very quiet, so I looked in only to see Nathalie bright red in the face, dressed in warm, tight woollen leggings, a warm top and bonnet, complete with warm booties. She was overheated and looked close to a heart attack – if that was even possible in babies. Jessica had outdone herself.

I stripped Nathalie down and gave her a cool bath, and not one peep from her. So long as Jessica was close by, she was happy. I spoke to her in English, but like Jessica, she would choose to reply in whatever word, in either language, seemed to suit the situation. Once we were out and about in the pushchair, Nathalie would study people who stopped to talk, then look at me as if to say, "What the heck?" Our family was now somewhere between English-Italian and gibberish when it came to communicating, but we seemed to get by. I was advised by informed family members that the girls would not progress at school, that they should speak the language of the country, which, of course, was correct. But I am happy to say they both went on to get degrees and have professional careers, and they are comfortable in both languages.

When the spring came, I was out on the bike, with Nathalie sitting in the front basket and Jessica on the little seat at the back. The shopping was tied to the handlebars with the girls' kindergarten bags on top of it. We would sing together, and wave to people as we rode past, but I did try not to stop too often as the entire arrangement and balancing act would come to grief.

When we all went to the beach or on a picnic, we would go on the scooter – none of us wearing helmets – with the same arrangement in place except that Jessica would stand up in front of her father, and Nathalie would sit between us, with me at the rear. Whatever we had to take along sat wedged at Franco's feet. The fishing rods could stand up at the back with Nathalie and me. On many occasions, by the time we got home, Nathalie would be asleep between Franco and myself. But when I was going to the markets, Jessica would walk beside me, with Nathalie in the pushchair. There was a handy tray below the seat that could carry quite a lot of shopping.

The fun days were taking the girls to the park that was very close to our apartment. We had a good gang and would meet up there regularly. Susan, Elaine and Toni were English. Karen was from Norway, Elizabetta from Holland, Ruzena from Czechoslovakia, and Lucia from the Lido. To fully understand what was going on with the children and their play was out of the question, because we were all trying to ensure our children spoke their mother tongue. Lucia was trying to learn English but threw her hands up in the air in the end.

18

A Trip to Albufeira, Portugal

Not long after I had settled in Venice, Judy, my close friend and former flatmate, had married her Englishman and moved to Portugal. We had stayed in contact over the years and during our exchange of news, Judy had invited us to visit. We took a flight from Venice to Madrid, and then changed flights to go to Albufeira on the Algarve Coast. Judy and Mike had two children by then, Mathew and Abigail. The differences in ages to ours were not that much, so the girls had playmates.

Their beautiful white villa with purple bougainvillea across the terraces was like a film setting. Not to mention the swimming pool. I recall that at this stage, our girls had not been in a swimming pool before. Nathalie was still quite small but had no fear of water. Her head seemed to operate on the premise – *If I jump, someone will catch me.* Poor Jessica, we had to drag her up from the bottom each time Nathalie landed on her. I think Franco and I finished up with wrinkled skin from the sheer amount of time we spent in the water.

The beaches were beautiful but the water quite cold compared to the Pacific and the Adriatic.

We enjoyed the restaurants, the amazing seafood, the beautiful Mateus Rosé wine and, of course, catching up. We did not participate in the crazy night life; I believe the partying along this coast is quite wild. We decided we were too old and had too many responsibilities at the time; we would do it next time! Unfortunately, there was not to be a next time.

By 1974, the Portuguese Colonial War was taking a stronger hold. It was a conflict lasting thirteen years, fought between Portugal's military and the emerging nationalist movements in Portugal's African colonies – Angola, Mozambique and Guinea-Bissau – between 1961 and 1974. There had also been a military coup in Portugal in April 1974, the so- called Carnation Revolution, and many people, like our friends, had to get out of the country in a hurry, and the beautiful villa was sold off for less than its value. The Carnation Revolution began as a coup organised by military officers who opposed the regime, but it soon gained momentum with the unanticipated uprising and support of the people. It was named thus since no shots were fired and people gave the soldiers carnations and placed them in the muzzles of their rifles. I believe it was a very scary, uncertain time, though, if you were seen as a supporter of the toppled regime. Our friends moved to Vancouver, Canada, and set up business again.

Our flight home to Venice from Portugal took us longer than a trip to New Zealand would have. The flight from the coast of Portugal through to Madrid was horrendous. As the plane approached land, it was as though it could not go any further. The winds were pushing us back. The flight was very rough and bumpy. We could not get a connecting flight to Venice either, due to poor weather, so we finished up in Rome and then headed on to Venice. With two children in tow, and all of us tired from the late night before, we decided that our travelling days were over!

19

The Friuli Earthquake

One evening in May 1976, while Franco was away at an Alitalia business meeting, I was getting the girls fed and into bed. *A night to myself,* I thought. I ran a hot bath and had just removed all my clothes when the apartment shook. The chandelier in the lounge was clanging as it swung back and forth. To feel an entire building, constructed of concrete and steel, sway and roll is terrifying. I heard screaming and shouting on the staircase. As I rushed to the apartment's front door, I picked up Franco's raincoat hanging on the coat stand and put it on. Outside, people were screaming, "Earthquake!"

Jessica had climbed out of bed and was standing by the bedroom door. Nathalie was stood up in her cot, her dummy getting a good workout! I took them both outside only to encounter sheer mayhem with the building's residents rushing for the gates. I quickly dragged Nathalie's pushchair out of the downstairs storage room, plonked her down, and off we ran. At this point I was feeling rather vulnerable due to my attire, but I had a firm grip on the belt!

We all raced up to the piazza that was just behind the seawall of the Murazzi. We were all very confident in the open space, but only because we did not realise that a tidal wave could be generate by an earthquake. The word 'tsunami' was not part of our vocabulary yet, and it did not become a familiar word until after we learnt of their occurrence in Japan. Cell phones were not around either, so I had no idea where Franco was except that he was on the mainland.

At about two in the morning people started talking about going home. The girls had been very good. There were other children running around, but they were all becoming very scratchy and hard to manage. We went home, and I was very relieved to release my iron grip on Franco's coat! I did not go to bed, however. I got dressed and prepared just in case there was an aftershock. The girls got into bed with me. At about three in the morning Franco came home to find us all sat upright, wide-eyed, with one baby dummy getting a bashing! Finally, the girls were placed back in their beds and Franco told me of the drama he had experienced.

The meeting had been held in a trendy bar on the mainland. When the earthquake hit, Franco saw an entire glass wall of shelves stacked with a vast range of alcoholic drinks just slip sideways to the floor and shatter. The Australian representative sitting next to him suddenly laid his head on Franco's shoulder, and at this point the entire building collapsed inward. Fortunately, no one was badly hurt but a few were taken to hospital for minor injuries.

We heard later of the devastating damage in the city and surrounds of Udine, which is further south of where Franco was. On 6 May 1976, just before 9:00 pm, the earthquake struck with its epicentre at Mount San Simeone near the town of Gemona in the Fruili Venezia Guilia Region in north-eastern Italy. The shaking lasted less than thirty seconds. But as it turned out, this was just a foreshock, having a magnitude of 4.5 on the Richter scale. After a short pause the mainshock struck. This time the shaking lasted much longer and was recorded as having a magnitude of 6.4. Udine was about 25 kilometres south of the epicentre of the series of quakes. Shocks and tremors continued for months afterwards, with a shock of 6.1 magnitude being recorded 24 kilometres north of Udine as late as 15 September 1976, for example. Besides Udine, many towns and villages suffered significant damage and losses due the earthquakes in 1976. For instance, the 6 May earthquake and its aftershocks affected 77 towns and villages, left more than 157,000 people homeless, killed 990 people, and left up to about 3,000 people injured.

Venice itself, south-west of the Fruili Region, was lucky as all that water in the canals acted as a buffer, absorbing the shock waves. We were told of the damage to boats on the canals crashing into the bridges, but the buildings were pretty much left intact. The tremors just kept on coming, not large ones, though, but the slightest feeling of a tremor played havoc on our already anxious nervous systems.

We continued living with this uncertainty right through to September. On one occasion I was out strolling, with Nathalie in the pushchair and Jessica walking beside me. We were on a small street with high- rise apartments on either side. To try to explain how I felt when the road beneath me bucked and rolled would sound like a fantasy. I did not know what to do – continue to my sister-in-law's apartment, which could collapse, or run for the beach. I chose the latter option, having no knowledge of tsunamis at the time.

I tried to get Jessica to run while holding onto the pushchair as we headed for the beach. Fortunately, I met up with people I knew and was able to wile away the time talking until Franco came home. The fear I had for the safety of my two babies far outstripped any fear I had for my own safety. Fortunately, the tremors stopped, but it took a long time to settle down my nerves. I do have to say we were so fortunate compared to the people of the Udine area.

20

Marital Bliss

The start of the summer was a very busy time in Venice. I had to prepare all the autumn and winter clothes, hats, leggings, coats, boots, raincoats, and so forth to be stored downstairs in our lock-up storage room, and all the summer wear had to be brought up, aired and sorted. Both girls had picked up a cold and sore throat and were at home, so this was the obvious day for me to do the job. The girls were free to play with all their toys, so within five minutes the house was a complete mess. At one stage we had half of the winter gear and half of the summer gear, plus the toys, scattered all over the apartment. I was completely happy until the doorbell rang. I answered via the intercom, thinking it would be the caretaker or the postman. Instead, it was Franco's older brother, Berto, visiting the Lido.

He ran the family hotels both in Cortina and in Feltre. Cortina is in the heart of the Dolomites, while Feltre is just to the south of the Dolomites, in the foothills. Consequently, we did not see a lot of Berto. I dashed around like a mad woman, stuffing toys under cushions, wiping the girls' noses, and trying to create some order to the piles of clothing. He arrived at the front door accompanied by a very attractive man of about the same age. I started with all the apologies – runny noses, sore throats, colds, change of season, blah blah blah. When I looked at my domestic chaos, I felt sick. Never in my life had my home looked such a shambles! I could imagine them thinking, *Lord is this how the English live? Poor Franco!* I could only try and explain the situation again. They sat on the couch as I prepared a Campari for each of them. I was really concerned when they sat down that there could be some serious damage to an area of their anatomy that they wouldn't have wanted to injure.

The other businessman was elegant, good-looking, and I would say, out of place! Berto, my brother-in-law, is a good guy. He was divorced and had never remarried. I was not sure about the status of the other guest, but I feel responsible for having put them both off marital bliss.

The girls' lives were very much controlled by the seasons, especially the complete change that occurred with each season. It was not only our wardrobes that were affected – it was a complete change of lifestyle. For the last quarter of the year, kindergartens and school ran from mid- September through to just before Christmas. As mentioned, the girls went to kindergarten or school either on the scooter or bicycle with their father or I took them on foot. In fine weather, Franco would often take Nathalie to her kindergarten on his bicycle in a little basket that attached to his handlebars, and I would pick her up in the afternoon. I would cycle with Jessica on the back and Nathalie in the front, and quite often with plastic bags of shopping and the school bags added. If you passed someone you knew, which was rather often, the balancing act became quite a skill.

All the young schoolgirls had a pink *grembiule della scoula*, a work smock that they wore over their clothes, and which reached to about the knee. Little boys wore blue grembiule. If it was a nice day when I collected the girls from kindy and school in the afternoon, we would head to the park. An entire group of *stranieri* (foreigner) mums, plus quite a few Italian friends, would flood the park. A small mobile bar and an ice-cream cart were conveniently close at hand, so we could indulge the children (and ourselves), after which the children were let loose to climb trees, play on the equipment, or just hang out. After the confines of the schoolroom, this seemed to be just what the doctor ordered! We mums would talk, relay dramas in our lives, report on our letters from home, share books, and, of course, relate any relevant issue regarding our offspring's health or lack thereof. This, of course, was when the weather was fine. Wet, rainy days were another issue entirely. Having children closed-up in our apartments when it was too cold or too wet to go out was our biggest nightmare. In our home, the time allocated to watching TV was approximately fifteen minutes for the girls. No iPads or gadgets were available then, only books and toys. I often gave a silent 'thank you' to Barbie! She could keep the girls happy for hours. Franco would sit at the table after dinner and make little figurines out of plasticine for the girls: a tiny priest, a few animals, a little dentist, Friar Tuck, and any popular TV personality.

By the time school broke up for the year, just before Christmas, the weather was cold, and the children all wore woollen hats and scarves, woollen stockings and little boots. Footwear had to be of the best quality and not cheap because the wet and snow rotted just about anything. We had to double wrap scarves over the top of each girl's coat, around the neck but under the hood. Of course, at this point, someone would always have to go to the toilet, which meant a complete strip down.

Our apartment was heated to about 23 degrees Celsius. I was always partly dressed as I would get into a real sweat dressing the girls. Finally, we could all go out. If it was raining or snowing, Franco would pick up essentials on his way home from work, or he would come home first, and I would go out to buy what was needed.

The back-to-school date was in the new year, well before mid-January. Nathalie had started kindy at four years of age, at a small convent called Campostrini, which was the order of the nuns who ran the school. Jessica had been there, so we were quite familiar with it, and Nathalie settled in very well. It was a little further away, but well worth it.

The end of March and the beginning of April is springtime in Venice. The huge old trees on Lido come to life, as do the great holm oaks, the huge magnolia trees, the willows, the poplars, the Lebanon cedars, the yews and pines, American mulberry trees, the wisteria, jasmine, oleander, and morning glory, gripping tightly with their colourful bells – it was all a wonder to behold. Fragrant roses abound in every colour, and American and Canadian creepers turn green again as they clamber up walls to reach for the sun. Going for a walk as a family along the canals with all the beautiful flowering trees and willows, and the masses of flowering shrubs along the banks, was always a pleasure. Add to this the incredible variety of architecture of all eras and styles, and the beautiful villas with their gated gardens, and a walk in Lido di Venezia was always a delight to the soul, no matter what the season.

With the spring we were out and about again, going to the park, shopping together, meeting up with friends for play dates, and finally back on the bike. This I loved. A group of us with kids and picnic baskets would cycle south to the other end of the island, to the small villages of Malamocco and Alberoni. There we would enjoy vast stretches of free beaches while we had our picnic lunches under a sun that was not too hot. The mothers just enjoyed the company and the long chats we had. The odd fight among the children was quite entertaining as we were all foreigners, and we all felt the absolute need to ensure our children spoke our mother tongue. So when these little ones would fight, mostly about sharing their toys, it would be in their home language, and mayhem ensued! Quite entertaining how the bad words were always learned from their fathers!

Spring was a changeable season and occasionally we would catch a heavy rainstorm cycling home. I'm convinced the Italians used to think, *There go those mad foreigners!*

21

Friends

Within our little group of friends, we were able to arrange play dates, afternoons in the gardens, and visits to the beach in summer. We would help each other out by babysitting. If one couple felt like a night out, one of us would look after the children, which was then reciprocated when the other family wanted a night out. This enabled us to keep up a lively social life, going out for dinners or for pizzas, but a very pleasant break either way.

If the weather was awful, we would take turns visiting one another's homes. Heavy fog was the norm in Venice in winter, and it could prevail for weeks. The apartments were all small, so our attitude was, *Let the children play; we can clean up later.* All the toys were set out, fights would erupt, food was always required, and the apartments became unrecognisable. As usual, we talked, shared books, exchanged information from home, discussed child-related problems, husband-related problems, and generally had a good time. We always followed the rule to be home in time to have the dinner underway, the table set, and the kids in the bath before their father came home, so in general we felt we were playing the game.

I had a little Fiat 500, which took the girls and me and our friends everywhere. Especially useful in the winter when it was cold and wet and for the kindergarten run. Some winter days we even had snow and temperatures below zero. Occasionally, a thick fog would descend over Venice, which, strangely enough, according to Venetian experts (that is, the mothers and grandmothers), made children extremely sick with sore throats, ear infections, chest infections – pretty much any infection could result from exposure to the fog, according to them.

The problem was that this little Fiat 500 was impossible to start. One of my passengers would invariably get out and give it a good push and off we went. I made noises around the husband that it should be looked at, but nothing was done. Then one day Franco rang. A colleague's girlfriend was coming to the Lido to do some business, and would I loan her the car? I had become used to having to call on friends to give me a push but failed to mention this in the conversation. I left the keys in the Fiat for her to collect and rushed off to the park to meet my friends. In my rush I forgot all about leaving a note to explain the pushing required.

She must have called Franco who told her I would probably be at the park, right next door! We all rushed back and gave her a push. Of course, on her return she had to find someone else to give her a push to get the car going. The deal was that Franco and his friend would come home together, and he and his girlfriend would stay for dinner. While I was rushing around trying to get the girls into the bath, the dinner started, and the house looking like a respectable home, she sat on the couch having the vapours. I fixed her a chilled wine and carried on. When the guys came home, half an hour was spent calming her down. She was still looking frail when they left.

The next day my car was in the garage! In the park, my friends and I discussed at great length the skills required to develop a fragile personality into something a little more robust. Still hasn't worked, even today. I do believe close friends are the answer.

22

Vinci and Montecatini

———————————

When the girls were still quite small, we did a tour with them to Vinci and Montecatini in Tuscany. The town of Vinci, which is located a little to the west of Florence, sits amid the hills of Tuscany at the foot of the Apennine Mountains. It is the birthplace of Leonardo da Vinci. The hillside town of Montecatini Alto and its companion town of Montecatini Terme in the valley below, are located between Lucca and Florence. Our friends Enrico (Rico for short) and Annamarie were living on the outskirts of Florence at the time, and he was doing business with the East. Franco had been friends with Enrico since they were about three years old. The couple had a son Marco, who was just in between the girls' ages.

Our mini breaks in this area of Tuscany have been very dear to us over the years. We have pictures of the girls and Marco in Vinci, at what has been called Leonardo's Tree. The story has it that the great Leonardo da Vinci would sit under the tree for hours, thinking and gazing across the valley at the expansive red poppy fields, the groves of olive trees, and the swathes of vineyards. We read his story to the girls and fudged an explanation for the word 'illegitimate' when they asked about it. We ate in the beautiful old town with its views all across Tuscany.

In Vinci, which dates back to the Etruscan Age, we visited the Museo Leonardiano, the Museum of Leonardo da Vinci, which is housed within the Castle of Vinci, also known as the Castle of the Conti Guidi (Guidi Counts). In the museum, full-scale models of some of the original inventions that da Vinci drew in his notebooks are on display, as are models of many of the tools he used. Across the road is the Biblioteca Leonardiana, the Leonardo Library, with a vast collection of manuscripts and drawings by the master.

The extend of Leonardo's genius is breathtaking and his inventions are well documented, but to actually be so close to the original notebooks and to be able to touch some of those tools and to gaze at the manuscripts, can only fill you with the wonder of it all. The very narrow, twisting streets and beautiful old houses of the town are the same today as they were in his day. I believe you are not allowed to hang out even your tea towels in Vinci, so as to preserve the dignity and authenticity of the place.

We carried on north-west to the medieval town of Montecatini Alto, built on top of a lofty hill overlooking the valley of the Nievole River. Today it is one of the most elegant towns in Europe, with its towers, medieval fortresses, massive walls, and churches, most of which date back to before the 12th century. At the foot of the hill is the town of Montecatini Terme, located in a place that was well known even during the Roman times for its special mineral waters. These are drawn from eleven thermal springs, all coming from the same source: an aquifer roughly sixty to eighty metres below ground level.

The town is built where once there was only swampland, which, although a breeding ground for malaria, also formed a natural defence, protecting the castle and fortification in Montecatini Alto. Montecatini Ferme has a turbulent history, including bloody battles and contested borders. It wasn't until the 16th century, when the Medici family started to drain and reclaim the land, and improve the infrastructure that it become safer to live in the base of the valley. Cosimo Medici, for instance, was the first person to build a dam and bridge to cross the muddy waters of the area. The Medici, along with the city of Florence, also allocated funds to restore the buildings belonging to the thermal baths that were already established there.

As time progressed, battles raging in the area almost reduced the town to rubble and the infrastructure also decayed considerably, to the extent that in 1772 the locks and weirs at Montecatini Terme were pulled down on the orders of Leopold, the Grand Duke of Tuscany. Then the channelling of unwanted water and the recovery of the thermal springs began in earnest, as did the restoration of the spa town. By the end the 19th century, Montecatini Terme had become a popular playground of the *Belle Epoque.* It was visited by artists, musicians, composers, and the rich and famous from all over the world. Giuseppe Verdi, Giacomo Puccini and Richard Strauss, to name a few, were regulars. The elite from all over Europe came to the spa town to 'take' the medicinal waters, particularly at the art nouveau Parco delle Terme spa complex.

Besides the beautiful gardens within the grounds of the many spas at Montecatini Terme, the town itself is surrounded by almost half a million square metres of magnificent gardens and parkland, sustained by the moisture and minerals below the surface. A stroll through the town with its ten spa complexes and collection of exquisite fountains, makes you feel as though you have been transported to a film set. In 2021, the town was declared a UNESCO World Heritage Site in the category 'Great Spa Towns of Europe'.

On the last trip we made there, Rico told us a story of when he had some Hong Kong businessmen in town who insisted on 'taking the waters'. The method is that you sit at lovely tables to enjoy a glass or two of the mineral water, but close by, behind a screen, are dozens of toilets. (You don't want to be held up here!) Rico sat with his guests, but they did not move. After a while, they suggested they should leave. Rico politely asked if they needed the toilet. They were fine, they assured him.

Just as they left town and hit the beautiful poppy fields, both guests turned pale and started calling out at the same time: "Lico, Lico, must stop!" They jumped out of the car when it was still running and took off across the fields. All Rico could see were two little dark heads in the distance, crouching low.

You do not mess with the waters of Montecatini Terme.

23

A Trip to America

Franco and I had agreed from the beginning of our marriage that if we wanted to travel, the girls would always come with us, fully aware that this might restrict our opportunities to travel. Franco's sister Bruna had married an American serviceman after the war and had moved to Detroit with him. Their daughter, Patricia, had visited us in Venice, but we had not met their son, Vincent, who was also married. The family had invited us to visit them in America, and our friends Elio and his wife, Pierina, decided to join us on the trip.

We had a two-night stopover in New York at the historical Roosevelt Hotel on East Street, just east of Madison Avenue in Midtown Manhattan. The grand hotel, opened in 1924 and occupying a full block, sadly closed in 2020. Our lovely accommodation and airfare were a great deal that we secured through Franco and Elio's Alitalia staff discount privileges. We would not have to scrimp and save on accommodation and risk such things as tummy bugs or dodgy backstreet deals.

We arrived in New York at 3.00 am and were in our room at about 3.30 am. The girls had slept well on the flight and were ready to play. Their passion at the time was Barbie dolls, and our girls had a plethora of them, including all the accessories – shoes, handbags, kitchen furniture, chairs and cars. These were all spread across our hotel bed. Four of us, plus all Barbie's paraphernalia, and Barbie on TV. Franco looked at me and said this is NOT what I had in mind for New York. The next morning, he woke up with a Barbie handbag scar on his face, some Barbie kitchenware digging into his back, and a grumpy face. As we became more confident on our travels, and the girls were a little bigger, we started to use the babysitting services available at the hotels!

On the morning of our first day in New York, we joined Elio and Pierina and hit the streets, which we could only describe as a shock to the system. Pierina and Elio lived in Venice, in a street very close to the Arsenal. It is a beautiful zone with housing very closely built, of course, and they knew virtually everyone on the street and would regularly chat with them. Having spent quite some time with the couple, we came to really love this part of Venice. People gossiped across the canals, stopped to talk on the bridges, and in this way, everyone was kept updated about matters. On the Lido too, even though it has roads and traffic, most of your day is spent on foot and certainly if you stop to talk to people, others are happy to walk round you and not complain. Not so in New York.

Elio and Pierina were as dazed by the city as we were. In New York we were afraid we would lose each other or one of the children. As soon as we could, we found a local breakfast place and sat down to eat. It was very like a local café in Venice; we noticed everyone there knew one another and they all talked together, and they all wanted to know which planet we came from! Even in a huge city like New York, we human beings gather around us the people we want to be with. Of course, we would have loved to see even half of what New York had as points of interest and attractions, but unfortunately, this was not to be that year.

From New York we flew to Detroit to join the family. Driving around became an issue as the girls had not seen traffic lights before, so they created a little song every time we stopped, which was quite often. Our agreement to always have the girls with us on our trips was wearing thin! Our nephew Vincent took charge of our trip and arranged excursions.

We visited the fairgrounds, another new thing for the girls, and we also exposed them to the great eating experiences in the USA. Vincent took us to see Niagara Falls. Poor Vincent. We all got close to being sent to jail during this trip. As a family, we travelled on Italian passports, so what should have been a quick look at the view from the other side of the bridge in Canada, became an incident. Vincent had assured us that although we could not enter Canada, we were allowed to cross the bridge to view the falls from the Canadian side.

However, we were stopped trying to cross the bridge. It turned out that the Canadians were very strict about this sort of thing. The Border Control officials pulled us over and had their firearms out, trained on us, as they came over to speak to us. One of the officials, a large, strong woman, seemed determined to have us arrested. Poor Vincent was beside himself as they read out the penalty for trying to get foreigners across the US border and into Canada. Italians required a visa even to cross the bridge, and we were without. They escorted us at gunpoint from the bridge. At least, while all the yelling and shouting was going on, the girls had the good sense not to say a thing! They allowed us to turn round and go back, with quite a few loud voices and waving arms to send us on our way. I know how I felt: embarrassed but relieved not to be in handcuffs. Jessica asked, "Why don't those people want us?"

Vincent and his wife, Dianne, lived in Florida, and he invited us to go back home with him. Vince and Dianne had a beautiful home in one of those magnificent housing estates that America does so well. The private barbeque area, the enclosed swimming pool, and the continual daily sunshine were to be envied. Like New Zealand, the young countries offer this space and ease of living. Old Europe, however, with its historical architecture and years of years of time to perfect its cuisine, culture and lifestyle, may appear somewhat tired in comparison, but it is always ready to give of its best to those who care enough to seek it out.

Florida was great fun and Disneyworld was a child's dream as, of course, it is meant to be. Nathalie was a little too young to make the most of the opportunity, but we returned a few more times in the years ahead, so she was able to experience it as a child as well. In fact, when we lived in New Zealand, we called in again, and the girls went on the giant Ferris wheel with their father. When they got off, I was waiting. Franco looked as if he was about to pass out, with his hair stood up on end and as white as a ghost. I was fussing and trying to get him to talk about what I could do to help. Later, when Nathalie had to write a report about her trip for school, she explained that Dad was terrified, and Mum was really concerned. Mum kept asking him if he was okay and what was wrong? Franco was not happy with the wimpy Dad image of him that she portrayed!

24

Transfer to New Zealand

We had decided to transfer to New Zealand. It was not an easy decision, but the political situation in Italy had become very unsettling. Every day some entity or another was on strike. You had to check on the radio each day to find out whether the public transport boats were going to be in service in Venice. Bread shops were closed on a Wednesday, butchers on a Tuesday, schools and kindergartens were closed on a Wednesday, universities on a different day, and so it went on. Small change was unavailable during cash transaction, so you were given sweets instead. It was not a very promising political or economic situation.

In 1973, the 'Ndrangheta, an Italian crime syndicate, kidnapped American oil billionaire J. Paul Getty's grandson, John Paul Getty III, and held him for a US$17 million ransom. Apparently, Granddad was reluctant to pay, but after receiving his grandson's ear, which his captors had cut off, he negotiated the ransom down to only US$2.2 million, which he reluctantly paid. Threats were rife in the political scene and businesses were going under.

Franco had applied for a transfer to New Zealand with Alitalia, but the airline only operated as far as Australia. He decided to apply to Air New Zealand for a position, and he was successful. Soon we had an appointment booked for our arrival in New Zealand.

We packed our possession into a shipping container, even managing to get the scooter in, and off we went. In New Zealand we stayed with my brother and his family until we found an apartment to rent. Within a short time, we had found a lovely large section and were talking to building companies about building a new home.

One of my promises to the girls (and to Franco) was that we would get a dog once we were in New Zealand as there was so much space on one's property. As soon as we were in our new home, off we went to the kennels and found a playful white Labrador puppy, whom we called Bepe. Bepe grew up to be a wonderful pet. Even when he was a little bigger, the girls could do anything with him so mild-mannered was he. One day he was dressed in a pink ballerina outfit with his tail tucked into the knickers. We had a long driveway to the road and the girls used to skate up and down it. This day they were skating up to the road with Bepe in tow, dressed as a ballerina. The girls came in for a drink and Bepe sat up on the driveway at the main street. Apparently, we were nearly responsible for a major traffic incident as cars were slowing down to look at this Labrador dressed for the stage.

He would lie still while the girls played dentist and patient, with all sorts of instruments put into his mouth. They even painted his nails with my nail polish. I would not like to say he was neurotic, but he hated going in the car, so we had to give him a doggy calming pill. On one trip we were going boating with some friends, and we stopped at a beautiful lake for lunch. Our friends had a little poodle. As we got out of the car, we found that Bepe was so drugged he was legless. We had to lift him out of the car and carry him to the edge of the lake, as our friends were doing with their dog. People having a picnic close by must have wondered why we had such a big dog if we insisted on carrying it everywhere like a small dog!

Jessica went to her new school in her lovely gabardine pleated skirt, leather shoes, and leather schoolbag but came home with a uniform list: nylon dress, plastic shoes, and plastic schoolbag. In a very short time, she had acquired a colonial accent, but was so happy to be anything but special.

Nathalie went to kindergarten once more. She was not as advanced as Jessica in English, but nevertheless, she chattered non-stop in Italian to everyone. Her philosophy was, *If you don't get it, it is your problem*! We decided to speak only English at home to assist the girls. We did get their English sorted out and they both went on to university, fully bilingual.

Years later when we lost Bepe, he was nearly eleven, and he'd had a great life. The girls wanted another dog, and they were at the stage where I thought I would be able to negotiate with them about it. However, this was one situation where I knew I was not going to win. The girls found a little Rhodesian Ridgeback left at the kennels, whom they named Conan. He grew into a very special dog as well. When Nathalie went off to university, she joined her sister in Dunedin, which was as far away from home as they could get, but so many of their friends were going there. Nathalie missed Conan and sweet-talked her father into getting him on a plane to go down and join them. Conan hated flying and made a fuss every time he was taken to the airport to fly home with them after each semester, and then back to Dunedin again. As you can imagine, both girls had Father in hand.

PART TWO

Barbara

25

Joining the Workforce

A TRIP TO ULURU

We had reached the stage where Franco was settled in his position at Air New Zealand, and the girls were happy at school and enjoyed exploring our new property. They had made friends with the local children and were inviting school friends home. For years I'd had the luxury of being a stay-at-home mum and now I decided to get a job. I found a position at one of the travel agencies in town, and when the girls' lessons ended, they went to their grandparents who were literally just a short walk from the school.

After about six months at the travel agency, I was offered an educational trip to visit the Outback of Australia. 'Educationals', also called 'famils' in the industry, were essential to ensure that we, as travel agents, knew what we were talking about when we booked people on tours. I was heading to Adelaide in South Australia, where our group would join a tour taking us straight through central Australia to the 'Red Centre' and to Uluru, or Ayers Rock, in the Uluru-Kata Tjuta National Park.

The tour started in Adelaide, with a stop in Alice Springs, and then on to Uluru. This part of the trip involved kilometre after kilometre of desert scrub, heat and flies, with the odd wildlife spotted from the road, such as kangaroos, emu, wild camels and dingoes. And yes, we knew there were dreaded, venomous snakes in the low scrub. The red reflection off the vast empty space put you into a trance of sorts. The barren, empty landscape has often been described as similar to that of the lunar surface, and I can certainly agree with the analogy.

We finally reached Uluru and our hotel. The massive rock loomed on the horizon for kilometres before you actually got to the little town situated close by. Our hotel was set in beautiful, seemingly tropical surroundings, with a grand entrance and a lovely swimming pool. Once we had unpacked, the group joined up and we headed for the pool. It was just before happy hour, and I was one of the last three into the water. While walking to the swimming pool, we noticed as we strolled among the trees that their branches were covered with thousands and thousands of bats. We all started to duck down and run for cover as hundreds of bats took off and flapped above us. Holding our small travel bags over our heads for protection, we ran like heck because it was so creepy. By then, we were all hot, flustered and bothered!

Once in the pool, we cooled off and enjoyed the water. Eventually, there were only two of us left in the pool. We two girls suddenly noticed a couple of huge wild pigs, with enormous tusks, at the pool's edge. The pigs were almost as large as bulls, in our opinion. Being the only ones left in the pool, we quietly dropped below water level to avoid their attention, but by the time we came up for air, they were in the water at the shallow end. We didn't know whether they might go for our legs if we tried to jump out, so we played at being submarines and kept slipping below the water while the bristly, scary guests continued to waddle in the shallow end! Luckily, they only wanted to get wet and have a drink; they were not there for the pleasure of swimming or exercising! As soon as we saw them preoccupied, we climbed out together in a second and headed for our rooms. Of course, the walk back through the trees also involved looking out for snakes in the grass. Australia has about 170 species of land snakes, some equipped with venom more toxic than any other snakes in the world. Later, we all set off on a walk with a guide. He advised us to keep to the beaten path because of snakes! Some of the girls needed the toilet, and at one point we came upon a tin shed which was the local loo! I was absolutely certain I was not going to go inside. The first poor lady who did, came rushing out with a scream, her knickers around her ankles and her handbag on her arm! When she could breathe again, and had retrieved her knickers, she told us that as she lifted the toilet seat, millions of little frogs started to jump all over the place. Apparently, they are drawn to water!

With bats in the trees, snakes in the grass, and frogs in the loo under our belts, we headed for the bar. A couple of drinks helped to calm our shattered nerves! The gin and tonic in the bar that night was bliss!

Early the next morning we were up to see the spectacular sunrise. The sun was like a ball of fire behind the massive rock, glowing and stark against the landscape. The view was surreal. It is very hard to describe that magnificent red colour of the sky at dawn in the Outback.

After a lovely buffet breakfast, we headed for the rock pools. We were told that freshwater sharks frequented the pools, but that they tended to keep away from noise! Yes, I learned that was a tall tale to scare the tourists, but crocodiles and thirsty snakes certainly do make their appearance in the Outback. Well, that took swimming off my schedule!

Some of the guys had great fun jumping from the rocks at the top of the gully into the pool, but we girls decided to give it a miss.

That day we did climb to the top of Uluru, a practice which has since been banned for cultural, safety and environmental reasons. People had been known to be blown off the top by strong winds, to slip and injure themselves, and to damage or deface the sandstone monolith. The site is sacred to indigenous Australians, the Aboriginal people. As a gesture of respect for their religious beliefs, cultural values and ancestors, the rock formation per se is now out of bounds to visitors. Some of the cave carvings and drawings at the site are the oldest known to man. It was hard work reaching the summit, but it was worth the effort. The view from the top was amazing, everywhere you looked there was desert as far as the eye could see. The sunset was quite breathtaking, a completely red sky that turned the entire landscape red as well.

The next day we headed north again, along the Northern Highway to Darwin. The landscape was desolate, very sparse in terms of living creatures and plants, but we did see quite a few camels. The rest was kilometres of desert. We arrived at the Kakadu National Park, an extremely beautiful, tropical area, and a UNESCO Heritage Site, covering almost twenty thousand square kilometres.

The park has a very high level of biodiversity. Creatures are found in crevices in every rock and tree, and in every river and pool, including insects, reptiles, birds, mammals and other fauna. The wildlife we encountered ranged from kangaroos and koalas to wallabies, cassowaries, crocodiles and dingoes – all roaming freely. The geological history of this area, well-researched by academics, goes back millions of years. The Aboriginal people are the oldest culture in the world. Their rock paintings have been dated back to forty thousand years in places, and their origin stories are recorded in the landscape and in their oral history.

We were invited to swim under a beautiful waterfall with a pool at the base. On doing a quick check, we found that freshwater and saltwater crocodiles like the pools in Kakadu, too! Some visitors went into the water because we were told that, generally, freshwater crocodiles are harmless to humans and don't usually bother you! We thought this information was unreliable. But saltwater crocodiles were a different matter altogether; they were always dangerous. Park and wildlife rangers constantly visit each pool in the region as the seasons changed to determine the level of threat, and they sign the area accordingly. But no thanks, we decided, and sat on the rocks instead.

While boating through the vast waterways of the national park, with beautiful water orchids floating by, we were told not to put our hands in the water as the crocs would take an odd bite!

Another gin and tonic at the bar that afternoon helped calm our nerves, as before. The return to our accommodation was yet another challenge. Towards evening the bats woke up and they darted around among the trees, and we were told they just love to get into your hair! Our return flight was uneventful, and I found it easy to slip into my domestic routine again. It was wonderful to be with our daughters, in our home, and in our garden that had nothing in it that could hurt you. I enjoyed being back at work in the busy travel agency, too.

I do have to say, that once home in our beautiful, lush country, I could relax. New Zealand is entirely snake-free, and except when in the bush, is largely frog- and toad-free. There are also far less flies than in Australia. In fact, a bush walk in New Zealand offers few hazards apart from getting lost along the less-worn tracks or taking a fall if unwary or exhausted. Among our native fauna, only the kiwi come out at night and these birds run away if there are humans in the area. Yes, we do have mosquitos in the bush and large eels in our pools, creeks and rivers.

My brother-in-law asked Franco if he was worried about me going off on these educational trips. Franco's reply was that he knew the woman he had married! I thanked him for that statement. However, he was in grave danger of finding himself married to an alcoholic. I believe you could become one quite quickly if you lived in an environment as dangerous as that which we experienced in Australia. We certainly felt the need for a stiff gin and tonic after some of the experiences we had there. We could have used the excuse that we were imbibing alcohol for medicinal reasons!

26

Our Neighbours in Howick

Over the years we had lived in Howick in East Auckland, and when the girls were still quite young, we had become friends with our neighbours Dr Hilary and Emily Moss, both well into their seventies. Hilary was British and Emily was from New York.

Hilary was a physicist and had worked with Oppenheimer on the Manhattan Project during the Second World War to develop the first atomic bomb. They had never had children, but Emily had been a schoolteacher and had taught swimming. Their property was a few beautiful hectares that included a lovely rock fountain with cascading pools and a swimming pool. They also had a regular cocktail hour, which was when we were invited for drinks and a swim. The couple became very close friends of ours; the girls became great swimmers, and we all took to cocktail hour! When Hilary and Emily had friends round, the girls were invited to help serve drinks and food. They became quite familiar with 'formal cocktail parties'.

One afternoon at about four o'clock, when I was in my kitchen, which looked out across the drive towards the entrance to their property, I noticed Hilary was out closing the huge double gates. This was very strange as they never closed them until six o'clock in the evening. I was soon to learn that sometime between 4 pm and 6 pm, when Emily came home, Hilary had committed suicide. He had been under hospital care for prostate cancer and had advised Emily that he would carry on with his treatment for as long as he could.

I went over to be with her and offer my support. The police were there and had taken Emily's statement. When they handed it to her to check what they had written, she managed to point out two spelling mistakes! (Always the schoolteacher.) We managed a little laugh. Emily sold the property and moved into a retirement village; she did not want the upkeep of the large grounds and house. When we visited her after she settled in at her new accommodation, she was always very chatty and cheerful. She had regular 'drinks' in her apartment, was on the committee of this and that, and continued well into her nineties. When she passed away, we had moved north to the Bay of Islands already, and did not drive down for the funeral, but friends told us they made it into a real 'bash', as Emily would have done.

27

The Girls Leave the Nest

Once Jessica had finished university, she decided she would do her overseas experience trip, her 'OE' as it is known in New Zealand, before getting into a career. This was pretty much a standard choice in New Zealand, a rite of passage for the young. Her first position was in England, working for Lord's Cricket Ground in London.

After that she worked on the super yachts operating in the South of France, where she improved her French. She wrote to us of one harrowing incident she experienced there. The yacht's crew had prepared food for sixteen guests, and at the last moment the owner said there was a change in plans, and they were all going out for dinner ashore. Jessica, in her wisdom, felt there must be loads of hungry people in the South of France. She loaded a huge amount of food into the tender and set off on her own. Once ashore, she dropped the food off at a shelter in the poorer area and had a chat with the staff. The risk of being harmed in that dangerous part of town was high, not to mention the owner of the yacht having her charged for stealing. Fortunately, none of the aforementioned happened.

Jessica was back in London when Nathalie made her career choice to be a photographer. After some research and experience in New Zealand, Nathalie was offered a position and an opportunity to study at a reputable photographic studio in Milan. As Nathalie's Italian was not as strong as Jessica's, it was decided Jessica would go over to Milan to help to get Nathalie sorted.

Two days later we had a call from Nathalie to say she was settled in the most beautiful convent in the centre of Milan! I was on the phone to Jessica immediately to ask how she managed to plonk her eighteen-year- old sister in a convent.

The decision, of course, was entirely logical. The convent, which accepted paying guests, was within walking distance to the studio. The meals were prepared for the guests and all their laundry was done. Nathalie loved the food and became a vegetarian. There were quite a few foreign girls staying there and the nuns were a lot of fun! We felt Nathalie was in safe hands.

How wrong can you be as a mother! The next we heard she was up a lamp post in the piazza outside La Scala with a ten-thousand-dollar camera, taking photos of a world-famous model. While I was on the phone with her, Franco was banging on about looking through our insurance policies to see if this was covered!

Nathalie had a great time. Ironically, she had to do a photo shoot in the Australian Outback for a top fashion company. Yes, at Uluru, Ayers Rock. She had with her a very elegantly dressed Italian photographer, fitted out in his designer clothes. They hired a van, and then headed off into the desert to reach their destination. Most of Nathalie's life had been spent here in New Zealand, so dirt roads, rough camping, and living in the bush was part of the general regime.

Her chief photographer had known only the design centre of the world, Milan. They were there to photograph a superexpensive watch on the arm of a little Aboriginal girl in front of the spectacular sandstone monolith. After doing all the driving, and protecting her senior photographer from flies, the heat, and the local people, she finally delivered him back to Milan. On her next adventure, she was sent out to photograph some cows! Of course, at the outset no one told her this was the plan. Off she went with her short skirt, suit jacket, and high heels to tread across fields, looking for cows. Each time she rang home after that, her father refused to answer the phone in case he got another earbashing about his fellow Italians!

Just before coming home to New Zealand, Jessica and Nathalie were together in Italy. Two of our friends who live there, Gianni and Piera, have two sons the same age as the girls. The youngest son had been to stay with us, so Gianni and Piera asked the girls to go skiing with them in the mountains in Italy. Neither of our daughters were experienced skiers because in the North Island we only have one mountain suitable for skiing, so it was not the popular sport that it was in the South Island. Off they went though, and the boys were told to stay on the low slopes with the girls, and not to take any risks, and so on. The girls told us that creeping along the beginners slopes was no fun at all, so they went higher up the ski field. There they took off, being the daredevils they are. Apparently, they had fun screaming down through the fabulous forests and snow runs. They did get the usual *blah blah blah* from us and were told they would not be let out on their own again, and so forth. You will be pleased to know that eventually they both did get home in one piece!

28

Meeting Barbara, 1980

With our contacts in Italy, Franco and I decided to start importing Italian decorative lighting. We found a supplier, two brothers in Treviso who ran Fabbian Lighting. I knew nothing about lighting at that stage, but found most people in the industry, such as architects and lighting engineers, were all very happy to answer my questions.

We soon expanded our business to include other decorative product lines. With a new set of beautiful catalogues shipped from Italy, I hit the town. Interior designers seemed to be a good place to start. I was given the name of a decorator to call on: Barbara Edwards Design. I made an appointment and popped in to see her. I did not have a business card and was obviously very green. I had been sent incredible catalogues and samples of exquisite curtain braiding, which I presented to her. She had a good look and then took out a pen. With a massive smile, Barbara wrote out an order for thirty thousand dollars, which was about the average annual income in New Zealand at that time.

This lady did interior decorating for hotels only, and the product I was selling was not otherwise available in New Zealand. I went straight home to tell Franco. He rang Elio, our friend In Italy, who then got in touch with a little shop in Florence, which produced the braid. This shop was originally the first stonemason shop at which Michelangelo worked as a student.

The next major order I received from Barbara was for a decorating project at another hotel in Wellington, for which we supplied three hundred bedside table lamps. I opened our first showroom in Parnell in Auckland, and the business grew.

Barbara and I went on a business trip to Fiji, where we supplied a block of apartments with lighting. We stayed with an architect friend of Barbara's. During the night, a huge Fijian man walked round and round the house and garden with a massive machete. He was the property's security guard.

We outgrew our first showroom and moved into a building in the Auckland CBD. The staff numbers went up. We employed two male lighting engineers, and had about four salespeople, plus a few reps on the road. I was able to get away only on short trips because the girls were still quite young. We did have a buying trip back to the lighting fairs, or exhibition as they are now called, in Milan, which was interesting.

I remember meeting a delegation of New Zealand businessmen there, and a shoe importer asked me to hold his hand. He had worked out that he was always looking down at what everyone had on their feet, while I was always looking up at the lighting. Therefore, this arrangement meant we would not fall over! I was also helping out as a translator on occasions. One day, back home in New Zealand, I had a phone call from Barbara saying she had an Italian property developer coming in from Fiji, who had a massive hotel project underway on one of the Fijian Islands. She invited the developer and his team of designers and consultants to dinner with me and Franco as guests, and as translators if required. Barbara and her husband, Graham, had the most beautiful home in Auckland. It had a massive entrance way, an amazing library, and a stunning swimming pool. They also had a major-domo, George, who assisted around the house. She decided to dress George up as the waiter to serve dinner that evening. We laughed as Barbara and I were both busty women, and we decided we would leave our top buttons undone to impress the guys. The husbands spent the evening pulling faces at us, and overall, the evening was fun.

Barbara was also talking about a big project for a hotel being developed at Angkor Wat in Cambodia. We were scheduling a trip there to talk to the developers. The next day I had a call from her secretary to say that Barbara had been taken to hospital. No one knew for sure what was wrong with her health at that stage. On the following Monday, she died from 'complications' that accompanied her condition. A close, medical friend of ours said that nowadays doctors could pretty much put all the patient's organs on life support until they found the problem. Nothing prepares you for such a shock. Her husband, Graham, and their family and all their friends were totally devastated. She left a very big hole in my heart, too. I still miss her today.

29

Brother Malcolm

While I was running our importing company, my older brother, Malcolm, had his own construction company, and occasionally we would find ourselves on the same project. I recall my first experience of this situation involved me going to site at the Ellerslie Racecourse in Auckland. I went straight to the site office, looking for directions. Inside, three workers were having morning tea, and in the background, on all the walls, were the usual illustrations of undressed women in every imaginable position. The guys rang Malcolm, and he was there in a shot. He gave the guys a real telling off and rushed me away. Apparently, he rewrote the rules as to where 'ladies' were allowed access on the site.

He was always there at the end of a phone call if I had any lighting- related issues or any other project-related matter I was not sure of. On one occasion we had brought in one of the largest Venetian chandeliers yet imported into New Zealand, and it was going to be fitted in a hotel in Wellington. The site manager rang to say they needed it on a certain date, which was sooner than they had originally asked for. He threatened to sue me or cancel the order. When I got home that night I was in a state, so I called Malcolm. He asked if I had put the date for the delivery on the contract. No, I had not. Had I confirmed any date with the site manager? No, I had not. "No problem," he said, "nothing can be done." The site manager did not have a leg to stand on. This was my brother – always calm, always informed, and always ready to help.

I knew he paid his staff on Thursday nights, but he kept the pay from the men. He would close off the building site on Thursday afternoon and buy the boys some beer. Then he would drive them each home and give the pay packet to the wife. He felt it was the only way he could thank the guys with a beer while making sure they would be at work in the morning, and also be certain the family had the money their menfolk had earned. On his retirement, the firm arranged a huge party at a lounge bar at the Ellerslie Racecourse. I was held up en route to the party, and I have often thought about that because punctuality was my thing, but I know the control I have over my emotions is practically zero and it promised to be an emotional event. I also know that Malcolm was not a person who enjoyed the limelight. The crowd was huge, and being in the same industry, I knew a lot of people who attended and was happy just chatting away until they called for speeches. This, I knew, would be Malcolm's moment of agony. He got through it; we both got through it. I don't think there was a dry eye in the house with all the accolades he received about himself as a person, as a boss, as a rock, and so it went on.

I felt like saying, "You guys have had him for his working life, while I have had him for my *entire* life."

Because of the structure of the family – first Malcom, then myself, only fourteen months younger, then Patricia, the baby of the family – he was always told to look out for his sisters. He would hold my hand to make sure I was safe. We would play in the hayfield at the end of the garden. Once, I managed to climb up a haystack to join him and our cousin Roy, and it was a lark to push me off. We would walk great distances through the woods, and I liked to pick daffodils, but that was not cool in his opinion. We climbed trees, then attracted ponies to the tree so that we could drop onto their backs for a short ride or, perhaps, get ditched in the river. I was party to it all, just as long as I did not complain or be a girl! Apparently, after one such excursion, my mother had so much trouble trying to wake me up after I fell asleep that she thought I had some dreadful ailment. She even held me up and spoon-fed me for a while. The doctor said I was just exhausted. Perhaps she could buy me a doll to play with instead, he suggested!

The adoration I had for my brother and our closeness carried on. I believe it was while we were on the ship migrating to New Zealand that some boys in the swimming pool insisted on tying my long plaits together and pulling them. I understand my father simply told Malcolm to go and thump them. Which he did. Never again did they torment me. Malcolm, however, did not have an aggressive bone in his body.

It was a happy childhood we shared. Apparently, one day Father suggested to Mother that he should go to New Zealand where there were more favourable prospects, a chance to secure a better life for the family, and that he should go alone and then send for us at a later date. My mother's reply was – *If you go, we all go!*

One of the delights of where we lived in England was that we could bicycle all through the woods, which were our back garden. So as a family, Malcolm had his own bike, my sister sat on a seat with Mother, and I sat on the seat behind Dad. We also used to take along our neighbour Kathy, who had lost her husband but had little Anita. It became routine that we would all go cycling together.

Finally, it was all arranged: we were going to New Zealand. It was a tearful goodbye with promises to keep in touch.

Once Malcolm had finished his apprenticeship in New Zealand, he declared he was going back to the UK and wanted to travel. I followed a year later, and we met up in Deal, our hometown in Kent. He had had a wonderful time touring with Bob, his mate, but Malcolm now seemed very settled. He had proposed to Anita, Kathy's daughter, and asked me to stay for the wedding. Malcolm took life very seriously. I noticed his back as he made his wedding vows. He gave such a big sigh that I thought his very flash-looking suit jacket was going to split down the middle! They sailed for New Zealand shortly after their marriage. I stayed on with Kathy. She had been a widow since she was about twenty-five years of age, and Anita was her life. Not long after, once Malcolm and Anita had settled in New Zealand and had purchased their new home, Malcolm arranged for Kathy to come out and live with them. Which she did.

30

Holiday in the Hauraki Gulf

We had friends with a holiday home on Great Barrier Island in the Hauraki Gulf, on the side facing Auckland. We had been invited to visit them but arranged a separate holiday accommodation. The area was a paradise, uncrowded and unspoilt, having so few residents, and it offered beautiful views and outstanding beaches.

One day Franco and I rented a couple of kayaks to explore around the rocky shore. We entered caves and felt like a couple of adventurers! Although, I doubt we were in more than three metres of water! We had a great morning, then sat in the sun and enjoyed the view. Later that evening, we went to the one and only pub with our friends for a quick pre-dinner drink. While there, we heard the locals talking about a young girl who had fortunately just missed an encounter with a shark.

Shortly after, in walked our daughter Jessica with her friends and everyone started clapping. I wasn't sure what was going on. Franco and I sat there like stunned mullets! Eventually the story got round to us. Jessica had been sailing on a friend's yacht and they were both in their diving gear in the water, collecting crayfish from around the rocks. Jessica was taking hers, secured in a sack, back to the boat when she saw the shark approaching, heading straight for her. She did the right thing: she put her body up against the boat, her back to the hull, and did not try to climb aboard. Sharks, I am told, would not attack the mass of the boat, but two dangling legs would have been a treat!

Thank heaven she knew what to do. Earlier, she had trained as a diver and had a holiday job taking tourist out to the sunken wreck of the *Rainbow Warrior* at Matauri Bay in Northland. This was the ship that had been bombed in Auckland Harbour by French government agents in July 1985. The *Rainbow Warrior* was the flagship of the Greenpeace fleet and was attacked to threaten those aboard who were protesting and campaigning to end nuclear testing in the wider Pacific, and on Mururoa Atoll specifically. After the wrecked vessel was refloated and the investigating into its bombing concluded, the ship was deemed unfit for sailing. It was towed north in 1987, where it was scuttled offshore close to Matauri Bay.

Interestingly, with the help of a local neighbourhood watch group, it took the New Zealand Police a very short time to identify and catch the offenders. It was on the news the following night. Someone saw their car leave the scene of the attack and drive away from Auckland, and they were sighted as they travelled north. Criminals don't seem to understand just how small New Zealand is. The offenders were soon picked up and detained: two French military operatives, acting under orders.

The Hauraki Gulf is very rich in human history and was one of the first places in New Zealand settled by the Māori people on their migration from the Pacific Islands. There are over a million hectares of sparkling blue waters dotted with emerald islands. Rangitoto, the youngest island in the Hauraki Gulf, is a dormant volcano. Its almost perfect cone shape is an iconic landmark as you approach Auckland City. Rangitoto erupted from the sea a mere six hundred years ago. It is covered mainly in black, broken lava fields. However, it has several hectares of pōhutukawa trees, known as the New Zealand Christmas tree because of its flowers that blossom bright red at Christmas time and its leaves that are velvety white, even silvery, underneath. Another wonderful island in the Hauraki Gulf is Waiheke, a leisure playground noted for its wonderful vineyards, art scene and exquisite beaches.

My sister, Patricia, and her husband, Tony, had purchased six hectares on Waiheke Island, on a hill overlooking the magnificent islands that fill this beautiful gulf. We had many wonderful holidays there, including many great parties – some of which were enormous – a couple of weddings, and loads of fun. And yes, we had adults behaving badly at times.

We had one of our holidays there during a time when mountain motorbikes were popular. Patricia and Tony have three boys, so they were well equipped to keep the young people happy. One night the four of us took off across the hills on these bikes. Tony and Franco were driving, and Patricia and I were just loving the buzz. The fact that it was pitch black outside, with the route following the hills and cliff edges, made it a real thrill. The next time the kids wanted to go out at night and do the same, it took them a long time to accept our refusal.

More than four hundred years before Christopher Columbus and the rest of the world worried about falling off the edge of the world, Māori people had travelled thousands of kilometres across the vast unknown Pacific Ocean in small ocean-going canoes and had become the first inhabitants of these islands.

31

A Short Trip with Patricia

TUSCANY

One year I headed back to Italy again to attend a lighting fair in Milan, and my sister joined me on the trip. It was great to have the company. Something I do love is sharing Italy with family and friends. As I'd done before, we found a hotel close to the home of our friends Lucia and Rico. They had a small dining room that seemed to be able to expand to enormous capacity, enough to seat and feed the number of guests present. Patricia and I secured a pair of bikes and off we went, visiting family and friends. The markets were always fun, but no matter how much you waved your arms around, you still had to speak the language to ask questions and make a purchase. Happily, I was then able to help. We did the tour to introduce Patricia to our English-speaking friends: Elaine, Tony, Susan, Ruzena, Astrid, Karim and Christine. Over the years, as one another's families had come to visit, we had all come to know them and to grow close, so it felt as though we shared this large, extended family. Lucia rang a friend in Milan who owned a magnificent villa in the Tuscan countryside. The three of us headed down, a girls' trip. The villa was spectacular, and it included a handyman cum butler. Bruno was all set to help in any way he could and just hung about, waiting to be of service. We all loved to cook and had decided the kitchen was too grand to ignore, and we wanted to produce a smashing meal or two. Bruno, however, was constantly there and seemed offended that we had simply jumped into his kitchen and taken over. When we were in the kitchen, he would bring out the wine and stand around, talking about his life and the war. Of course, he did not speak English. We soon developed a 'Dodge the Butler' routine. We would let him know that we had had a hard day and that at seven-thirty we would like to go to bed and read.

We also skipped into town for lunch, and in the end, we explained we had dietary problems and suggested we cook for ourselves. All we wanted was to have some privacy and to talk to one another. When we sat round the pool, we could quite easily grab our own towels or a cold drink, we explained as well.

It was obvious we were not his usual class of resident. After a full day of sightseeing in the surrounding area, we were simply content to go home, have a swim, and chat all night.

While in Tuscany we visited Assisi, which is almost in the centre of Italy. In his *Divine Comedy*, Dante plays on the name of St Francis's birthplace. Dante's metaphor in his masterpiece compares St

Francis to a 'sun'. He wrote: "a sun was born into the world", and he transformed the name Assisi to *Ascesi*, which means 'I rise' in Italian. And then he says even Ascesi is too humble a name for the saint's birthplace, that one "would name it [more] rightly" if he were to call it "Orient", which means 'East', the exact place where one sees the rising sun on the horizon. This is fitting since St Francis's legacy, and the light which emanates from him, has illuminated and warmed each generation for seven hundred years.

There are numerous books on the life of St Francis, the son of a rich merchant who abandoned his family to live in poverty, caring for the poor and administering to the lepers who were abandoned to live in caves and miserable huts. We visited one of these caves and realised the horror of what it must have been like living there in the middle of winter. We tend to think of St Francis as dressed in rags, preaching to the poor and feeding the destitute, and of his great love for animals. But when you look back, you learn that he was so much more and had a wider impact. His excursions abroad were many. For instance, from 1219 to 1221 he was in Egypt, trying to convert the sultan, al-Kamil, and put an end to the conflict of the Fifth Crusade. He also travelled to Rome and Spain. He founded several religious orders, including the men's Order of Friars Minor (the Franciscan Order), the women's Order of St Clare (the Poor Clares), the lay Third Order of St Francis (the fraternity of Brothers and Sisters of Penance), and the Custody of the Holy Land priory in Jerusalem. He attracted a huge following and had an influence on a vast number of religious entities. Besides being deeply involved in establishing and administering his various orders and in caring for the monks and the nuns, he also spent significant time preaching, writing and praying.

You cannot explain the reverence you feel while in his cave near San Damiano, and at the Porziuncola – the small chapel of Saint Mary of the Angels on the plain below Assisi, and at the Basilica of Saint Francis of Assisi. Merely being in this beautiful medieval town and its surrounds was a profound experience. After sightseeing in Assisi, we collected our car and drove back to the villa. We had so much to see, and a visit to Florence was at the top of our list, but that would have to be on another journey at another time.

Back at our lovely villa, we just soaked up the tranquil atmosphere and enjoyed the cool water of the swimming pool. Relaxing at the end of the day, we had our usual aperitif and yes, just gazed out across the beautiful poppy fields to the distant hills with the odd castle to left and right of the landscape.

32

Jessica Comes Home, 1991

———————————

We had a call from Jessica to say she had decided to join some friends and was coming home through India. At Mumbai they were all going in different directions, and Jessica had a bus connection to get to Delhi. We were thrilled and looking forward to catching up.

Jessica was prepared for the bus trip. She had picked the front seat behind the driver, had her headphones and a good book on hand, and was in no rush. Once up in the hills, the roads became very narrow and steep, with massive drops down one side and close mountain walls on the other. There was a tour group aboard the bus. Among the tourists, Jessica had noticed an elderly couple with a severely handicapped daughter who must have been in her thirties, and who they were having difficulty managing. They were Italian and had exchanged a few words with Jessica. As the journey progressed towards late afternoon, their bus turned a bend and ran into a loaded-down truck.

Everyone started screaming. The Italians because they were trying to cope with their daughter. Jessica tried to offer some help to quieten the desperate mother. From then on, they clung to her as they did not speak English at all.

The police arrived and started to take control. Apparently, the daughter was in dire need of medication, which they had run out of. Jessica was asked to go down the hill to the village pharmacy to buy the necessary sedative. Running back up the hill in the dark, medicine in hand, a police officer started chasing after Jessica with bad intentions! When she came home, Jessica told us about the choice words she hurled at him. I was not aware she knew such language! However, he did back off and she was able to help the distraught family.

Late in the night help arrived, and they were all transported to the hotel.

Once at the hotel, both the tour leader, who had done very little to assist the family, and the elderly couple asked Jessica to meet them for breakfast so they could thank her properly. Jessica declined and went to her room and rang her father to have him arrange a flight home for her via Sydney. Since Franco was working for Air New Zealand, it was easily done. We were very relieved to have her home and I must say very proud of how she conducted herself.

33

Jessica's Twenty-First Birthday

Jessica had decided she wanted a fancy-dress party at home for her twenty-first birthday celebration. The theme was 'come as a famous person in history'. We had cleared the garage to create a space for the guests and for dancing, and I had spent days shopping and arranging for the food required. I ordered a large roast beef along with roast chickens, plus all the salads. The fresh vegetable would come from the garden. The cake was delivered, the music installed, the neighbours advised, and we waited for our guests. They had outdone themselves! Our male guests included a Māori chieftain, Gandhi, Churchill, Einstein, Hitler, and a Roman gladiator, with many other well-known historical figures represented. The female guests included the Queen of the United Kingdom, Mrs Thatcher, a Māori princess, and Amelia Earhart, among others, along with Nathalie as Greta Garbo and Jessica as Catherine de Medici.

It was a great night. To prevent any accidents, we had arranged for our guests to sleep over, having 'confiscated' the keys to their vehicles. To this end we had erected tents in the garden, boys' tents and girls' tents separate, of course. Naturally, the young people talked and giggled throughout the night. I am not sure what time it was when I found myself stood on the top balcony in my white nightdress, threatening them with hell if they did not quieten down and go to sleep. The next morning they all said that I looked like the Angel Gabriel standing there in my white garment. What was coming out of my mouth, though, would not have been understood by the Angel Gabriel himself !

On another occasion, Nathalie had been invited to a party further out of town. Since I knew most of the kids, we agreed to her going and transport home was arranged. Franco was working nights and was on duty that evening, so when I got the phone call from Nathalie at one in the morning to please come and get her, I did the usual rant: "What about your lift that I arranged?" and so on. She just kept asking that I please come and get her. As the roads were completely deserted in the beachside area where we lived, I simply threw a cardigan over my nightdress and took off. On the way to collect her, my mind composed hundreds of things I was going to do to her, including grounding her for a month and no more parties. When she got into the car, I started up, but Nathalie, being who she is, began to tell me some very funny stories. Obviously, her brain said, *Keep Mum laughing, and she will forget to admonish you!* We laughed all the way home, and I'm still not quite sure how that happened.

34

Nathalie and Martin

After returning from Italy, Nathalie joined a well-known photographer in Auckland as an assistant. This was adream job for Nathalie because the project she was assigned was a book on animals. Nathalie is the ultimate animal lover. Obviously, she was not taking photos of cows in fields, of which we have millions. This time the photos were of individual animals, including dogs, and were very special photos. Dogs being a passion of hers, I think she found the project to be a real joy. On one of their trips, Nathalie and the photographer went to a zoo in Australia, and we have a photo of Nathalie sitting beside a huge white lion. What we could not see was a behind-the-scenes guy who had a massive chain pulled tight around the lion's neck! I loved the photos of the little cubs!

Along with this job, she was also doing weddings across the North Island. Her eye for detail was a gift, one that was certainly not handed down from me. Perhaps a talent inherited more from her father.

With Nathalie's birthday being on Christmas Day, we always had to find ways to acknowledge it and celebrate it as a separate event. Jessica was very determined that Nathalie should not miss out when it came to her twenty-first birthday! I usually tried to have her friends for lunch and the family for dinner, or the other way round. I was not allowed to use the Christmas theme either. So the pattern developed over time.

I would prepare the lunch table, I recall, all in pink or blue, with decorations and a lovely tablecloth and so on. On this day, her twenty- first birthday, the decor was all powder blue. But as a surprise, I had her birthday cake made in the shape of her very special dog, Conan, our Rhodesian Ridgeback, and the finished product was so lifelike. The cake experts had done a wonderful Job. We hid 'Conan the Cake' in the cupboard so Nathalie would not see it before the celebration. However, when it came time to cut the cake and sing Happy Birthday to her, Natalie would not let anyone touch her 'cake Conan'! No way! I had to run around and serve the guests some other dessert. All her friends agreed – it was too good to cut.

The friends hung out and danced and had a great time, then went home. By this time, I was well into preparing for the next sitting, with the family coming over for Nathalie's birthday and our Christmas celebration. A red tablecloth was set, arranged with Christmas decorations. The family started to arrive. I think there were fifteen guests, plus us four and the girls' boyfriends. Yes, they all loved Conan the Cake, but again, he was not cut up. We did all the twenty-first photo shoots, including many with Conan the Cake and the real Conan. Nathalie said that when she felt she was ready to cut him up in his cake form, they could all come back and enjoy a slice!

At this stage, Nathalie was going out with Martin, who had been her close friend from a very early age. Martin lived just down the road from us, with his three sisters, one of whom is his twin. The friendship between him and Nathalie grew around their love of dogs. Martin had a little pug, Ramone, full of mischief, and we, of course, had Conan. The two dogs were great mates. When Martin went overseas, and Nathalie was away training, I had the pleasure of looking after these two, which had its moments.

Martin's parents owned a beach house on one of the most dangerous beaches on the West Coast. It has black sand, rugged hills, and enormous waves almost all the time. His family spent a lot of time there, and Martin was and still is totally at home surfing in these massive waves. It was here that he proposed to Nathalie.

On a visit with them to the beach house, Franco and I had been given a cabin set back in the bush behind the house. The boys were going to watch the rugby, so I was happy, or so I thought, to remain in the cabin alone in the thick bush. During the night I needed the bathroom and the cabin had none, so there was really only the bush as an option since it was way too dark to clamber down the hill to the adjoining house. Managing my white cotton nightdress and the torch was daunting as it was pitch black outside. Finding somewhere to put my feet without getting prickles and cuts was a real issue. I decided I was not really a bush girl. I also kept out of the sea as there had been shark warnings. The gentle, soft Adriatic beaches came to mind, with some nostalgia.

Piha Beach

35

Visiting Italy with Heidi, 2018

VENICE AND FLORENCE

I had to go back to Italy on business again in 2018 and Franco was not very keen on the trip, but we had been talking about our granddaughter Heidi coming with us on one of our visits to Italy. I could not let Heidi down, so plans were soon underway for the two of us to make the trip. She had not been out of New Zealand before, making the trip a big adventure from the start. Heidi and I flew to Dubai first, which blows your mind after leaving Auckland, a fairly modest place in comparison! Heidi travelled well. She slept without a problem, listened to music, and watched the films available. You would think she had spent her life on planes. The chaos of Italian Customs at the airport did not seem to worry her. I used to get very uptight about this each time we went to Italy, but Customs seems to have changed their systems, and it is less onerous now. We were met at the airport by our friend Elio, who, as mentioned, had worked with Franco at Alitalia. In fact, they had joined the airline at the same time and had trained together in Rome. Elio took us from the airport by speed boat, travelling right up to his front door in Venice. He had a lovely old villa with an inner courtyard. His daughter and her family lived in the courtyard cottage, his brother-in-law and his family lived on the first floor, and Elio had the top two floors plus the roof garden to himself. As mentioned earlier, he had lost his wife, Pierina, to cancer, which had devastated the family. There was one spare bedroom on the first floor and another guest bedroom just under the roof garden.

The stairs at the villa were steep, and, after running round Venice all day, we were certainly not sprinting up the stairs. Heidi enjoyed the company of Elio's daughter Caterina and his son-in-law, Zokol. They were both musicians at La Fenice Opera House, as mentioned, and played in beautiful locations round Venice. They took Heidi to the beach at the Lido, and they all had fun dealing with the language issue.

Elio kept his lovely yacht just around the corner from the villa, so day trips were convenient. We enjoyed sailing round the Venetian Lagoon and showing Heidi all the sights and pointing out the various islands. We sailed round behind Guidecca Island to the Cipriani, a world-famous hotel, and enjoyed its magnificent gardens. We also visited San Giorgio Island with its beautiful Church of San Giorgio Maggiore. Franco went to school on the island of San Giorgio, and we looked for his classroom at the school and told him his name was there, listed among those who had failed! (Which, of course, was not true.)

Rico and Lucia arranged for the four of us to take the Red Arrow, the fastest train in Europe, to Florence to show Heidi the beautiful city. We had just settled on the seats when Rico asked Heidi whether she liked travelling by train. Her reply was that she had never been on a train before. We only had one mainline passenger service in New Zealand's rail system, so we travelled everywhere by car. It was fun rushing through the countryside at 500 kph.

Bruno, an old friend of both Franco and Rico's, picked us up at the station in Florence. He and his wife, Benji, had hotels in the area, so our accommodation was very pleasant. Heidi and I shared the attic apartment, which had magnificent views of the surrounding Florentine countryside. The swimming pool was Heidi's first stop, which gave me a chance to spend time with Benji and Lucia. We have known each other a long time, and it is so strange the way you can sit down and almost pick up where you had left off, even when you have not seen one another for quite a while.

Benji was great in terms of the local markets and trotted us around to all the best ones in Florence, and there were quite a few. Bruno took us all sightseeing, followed by another beautiful lunch in Vinci. Heidi spent a lot of time looking for gifts for her classmates. I tried to help her draw up a budget, but Heidi had been working on it in her head already. She had allocated a sum and then managed, between Florence and Murano in Venice, to purchase a little gift for practically every one of her classmates. I found she was also a good people-watcher. In one of the restaurants we visited, Bruno and Rico were engaged in a deep political dialogue, and Heidi was sitting to the side. I said that I was sorry we were not included in the conversation, but that was useless to try to interrupt Italians. She replied that she had been watching the people at the next table, the conclusion being that one of the guys was a complete control freak. We agreed we were not into that sort of person!

Heidi and I were at the Guggenheim Museum in Venice when we got the call from Paola, my niece. Her mother, Franco's sister Lilly, had died that morning, at the age of eighty-seven. Heidi and I had been at their apartment only a few days earlier. She had just been brought back to Venice from Padua, the location of a top medical facility in Italy, and now arrangement were being made for her funeral.

Lilly and Lino had lost a son, Guido, when he was only fifty years of age. He was a brilliant professor, a great musician, and a man passionate about sailing. In fact, he had been in Madrid to see Spain prepare to compete in the America's Cup, and he had rung us at home to say he was going to come out to New Zealand for the America's Cup Final. His death devastated the family and the university and all his friends. He was brilliant, extremely handsome, and real fun to be with. His English was excellent too, so I could not get away with anything where Guido was concerned. He was buried in the family tomb in Venice on San Michele Island.

Lilly was going to join Guido. We sat with Lilly's coffin on board the funeral barge. The trip across to the island was not very far, but it was an incredibly hot day. We gathered under the trees while they opened the tomb to prepare for Lilly to join her son and her husband's ancestors. Her two daughters and husband and grandson were there to say goodbye. The Cemetery Island, with its age-old trees that have been standing in attendance on the dead, among which some of the world's most famous people, is very beautiful, though an atmosphere of enduring sadness prevails.

36

Boating

Besides the various types of boats used for public transport in Venice, there are, of course, the small privately owned runabouts or speed boats. They are literally used the way we use cars in New Zealand, and the traffic rules that apply are also very clear. On one occasion, during one of our many trips back to Italy, a friend offered to take us for a boat ride through the canals of Venice. We decided to prepare a picnic for this excursion.

When it came time to enjoy our late-afternoon picnic, we tied up under a bridge, but right in front of a 'No Parking' sign — as you do in Italy. We had just started putting the food out when we heard, "Hey, Giacomelli." It was one of Franco's old mates, who couldn't believe it was him, back in Venice. A grand dialogue ensued. Shortly after, another "Hey, Giacomelli" came from someone on the bridge. Franco was happily talking to his old mates while the rest of us got the food organised.

Next thing, the cops arrived. First, they asked us if we could read. There we were, having a noisy picnic under a 'No Parking' sign. We packed up and carried on through the dark canals until we found another 'No Parking' sign under which to finish our supper.

Because you have to walk almost everywhere, Venice is really a close- knit community. When you pass the same person every day, you do come to feel that you know them. Also, you would very often find that your mother or father grew up with that person, so you automatically say good morning. Basically, a quick walk through town was a continuous litany of *"Buongiorno"*, *"Salve"*, *"Ciao"*, or *"Buonasera"*.

I would say to Franco, "Who's that?"

The answer, for example, could be: "Beppe, Auntie Maria's brother, Roberto's cousin." In the end you throw your hands in the air. I recall one elderly lady stopping us to talk to "Franchetto", the diminutive version of Franco in the Venetian dialect. She had known him since the day he was born and still recognised him on the street. So even with all those thousands and thousands of tourists, the small-town community still lives on, hidden within the masses.

37

The Sporting Connections

RUGBY, 1989

We had not been settled back in New Zealand for long when Franco received a late-night call from our friend Gianni, asking if he could find a couple of good All Blacks to go and play rugby for Treviso, just outside of Venice. Franco laughed. "Does Gianni think I keep them under the bed?" were his words. We had no contacts in the rugby world. A few enquiries later, however, and we were directed to the Pakuranga Rugby Club, which was not too far from home. After many phone calls, Franco gave Gianni a few contact numbers. This was the start of a strong bond between New Zealand and the Benneton Rugby Club, also known as Benetton Treviso, in Italy. Incidentally, Gianni was the freight forwarder for all Benetton's products worldwide.

On one occasion when we were in Italy, Gianni suggested we all go out and take the All Blacks with us. Franco pointed out it might be cheaper to buy them each a new suit! Nevertheless, we did so and went to one of the incredible palatial villas that sit on the banks of the Sile River just outside of Treviso. We had a great time, stretching Gianni's English to the limit.

Soon after we returned to New Zealand, we had a call from an Italian gentleman who had been given Franco's name as a person to contact in Auckland. He expressed a real desire to visit a typical Kiwi rugby club. Franco scratched around and found that the Pakuranga Rugby Club would be happy to host him for the day. We met the gentleman and his wife and daughter at Auckland Airport. The next day we took him to the club. We thought he was going to kneel and pray. He seemed to be in awe of the 'Great Giants' and the rugby cups on display. He was excited about the trophies they had won, the photographs of the teams and players; it was incredibly emotional.

When we parted a few days later, he shook hands, almost in tears, and said, "I will never ever remember you!"

Observing our expressions, his daughter said, "Dad, it's 'I'll never ever *forget* you'!" On that little giggle, we said our farewells.

With all the buzz going around at the time of the 31st America's Cup held in Auckland in 2003, contested between the holder, Team New Zealand, and the winner of the 2003 Louis Vuitton Cup, Swiss challenger Ernesto Bertarelli's *Alinghi*, general chatter seemed to be all about the same topic: Can we beat the Italians? Friends had invited us to join them on their launch to observe one of the race events. There was to be quite a group aboard. There was one caveat, however: Franco was not to cheer for the Italians. What they did not know was that the Venetian dialect, and especially Venetian 'bad language', is just about impossible for anyone else to understand. So he did let rip in a colourful way. There were moments, though, when he did say "Bravo, bravo!" to the Kiwis.

The after-party was great, as everyone who lived in Auckland at that time remembers. Sadly, I had missed a wonderful opportunity a week before the races, due to my vanity. I can't remember why they did so, but my staff at the time had given me a gift voucher for a luxury facial treatment at a spa in town. Not something I usually partake of. It was Friday night and by the time I had finished, I was desperate to get back to the car. The parking ticket was about to expire. So I left the clinic with my face aglow and no make-up, as greasy as you could imagine. Running through the dark streets to my car, I felt confident no one would even notice me. The next moment, I heard my name being called. It was Mario, our Italian Consul. He was just off to the pub to meet Team Luna Rossa, and could I join him? I declined due to my greasy hair and oiled skin, and so forth. He kept insisting, but there was no way I was going to walk into that flash pub to meet those gorgeous guys looking like I did. I think I swore all the way home.

38

Franco's Seventieth Birthday

Before moving to Kerikeri in Northland, Franco had his seventieth birthday coming up, and I decided a nice surprise would be in order! So the planning started. Invitations were sent out with only my number to reply to. The girls and I spent many happy hours planning in secret. The one secret I did keep rather well was that I had invited two of his closest friends in Italy to come out to New Zealand for the celebration. Elio, unfortunately, had his father in hospital and could not leave him, but Gianni and Piera agreed to come. I had clandestine meetings with caterers, florists, the booze shop, and so on.

The day Gianni and Piera arrived at the airport in Auckland, I took Vaughn, a young man who worked for us, along with me to pick them up. They were booked in at a motel near our home, and I agreed to collect them after work to take them out for dinner. I told Franco I had a meeting with an interior designer! And so the lies started. I arranged for all the booze to go to neighbours to be stored until the day of the party. The caterers had to deliver the food to the neighbours as well.

During those last few hours before the celebration started, I created drama at the showroom, a situation that Franco had to address, so as to keep him from coming home. While he was attending to this, the tables were set up at our house, and huge bouquets of flowers were arranged in the lounge, with the door to the lounge kept closed. I had told Franco it was just the family coming over for his birthday.

Nathalie's husband, Martin, came round with all sorts of sound equipment, which he told Franco he was getting some help to fix. Franco tried to help him but was rebuffed. The house had a large conservatory on the side that faced the driveway. As we saw friends start to arrive, I asked Martin to put on the music we had selected – Wagner's 'Ride of the Valkyries'. Of course, that stupendous sound brought Franco into the lounge to turn down the volume. When he looked up, we had about forty people walking through the door! It was chaos. Then we all stood back as his friends from Italy walked in. Introductions were off for the day! They were all shaking hands and hugging; a common language was not necessary. We had the Italian Consul carving the ham with all the pretty young girls helping him. I have to say, I had done my bit, and the rest just happened naturally.

The next day I told Franco I could start an affair at any time, and he would not notice. I had been out to the airport, I had meals in restaurants, I had taken Gianni and Piera out and about, and he had not had a clue. He simply gave me a big hug. I guess that was all that was needed.

Cousins

39

My Seventieth Birthday

It was coming up to my seventieth birthday and we were very busy at work, so I had not planned on doing anything to celebrate the occasion. Franco and the girls made noises about us going out on the day to one of the beautiful wineries we have here in our part of the North Island. It would save me a lot of effort!

While at work on the morning of my birthday, I tried to pop over to the shops a couple of times, but each time someone stopped me and insisted they go instead. I carried on working until lunchtime, then we left the staff in charge and the girls took me home for a quick freshen up. Franco was in the kitchen, but the girls kept rushing me out for our booking at Marsden Estate.

As I walked in the door of the restaurant at the winery, I was faced by my entire family. Aunties, cousins, my sister and her family, my brother and his family. I think we were about thirty in the party. For once, they told me, my mouth was shut. It was mayhem, as we are a vocal lot. We had drinks outside under the willows and then sat down to a buffet lunch. It was great. The after-party was to be back at our place, and this was catered as well. It was a gorgeous day.

I found that the family were all staying in motels around town, and that was why each time I attempted to leave the showroom I had been stopped. I could have bumped into any one of them on the street. A bus had been arranged to pick them all up from our home and take them back to their motels, but that was way later. The music went on and we were dancing well into the night.

Normally, with a party at home and the lake being only a few steps from the terrace, children's safety was always a concern. This time, however, one of the adult guests just happened to slip off the end of the jetty and into the water. The friends gathered around and managed to find something in my wardrobe for her to wear! It was a great night.

The next morning, the guests were all back, and they helped us with the clean-up Everyone was saying what a great house party it had been, which reminded me of one of my own stories. I have never been much of a baker, and I don't eat much sweet food. However, one day I made an effort, and I baked an apple pie for the girls' afternoon tea after school. Neither of them are big on cakes either. My poor attempt must have done a couple of kilometres around the kitchen before I decided to put it on the edge of the lake for the ducks to eat.

Not long after I did so, I left the kitchen to go down our long hallway, and I found a family of ducks inside the house, looking as though they were off to the bedrooms. With horror I noticed they were 'pooping' as they went. Fortunately, we had tiles on all the floors! I chased the ducks out of the house. I was telling the girls about this, feeling guilty that I had poisoned the ducks, when they noticed the ducks had not touched my apple pie. It is still a great laugh for the family when it comes to my pie- making skills. Even the ducks won't touch the pies I bake! As they said, goodness knows what bowel trouble they were having!

40

The Golden Sands of Change

When I look back, I see my life as one of almost continuous change. I remember the pale golden sand dunes that went on for kilometres on the western shore of Lido di Venezia. They, too, were subject to change. While the wind, the weather and the light ensured the view across the dunes was never the same, the dunes themselves endured, steadfast and familiar. From my initial meeting with Franco in England, and the travels we did between countries, to us each settling in a new country, our views of the world have changed, too. First there was me settling in Venice, Italy, and then Franco and our children coming out with me to New Zealand, where I had grown up, and us settling here as a family. It has been a significant adventure.

When moving to a new country, you suddenly find you are an island until you learn to speak the local language. The need to communicate drives you to look for company among those who are in a similar situation, or with whom you have something in common. Fortunately for me, I happened to meet such people very quickly in Venice. Franco had many friends who, like him, had met and married women of other nationalities. These friends became my lifeline and eventually led me to develop a deep love for Italy. As we transitioned from young couples with young babies, to more experienced parents and mature adults, our circle of friends expanded. Once kindergarten and school were on the agenda, we all made new friends with young Italian mums and dads, and so our world expanded yet again.

When Franco joined Alitalia Airlines, our lives changed once more. We were able to visit countries I had never dreamed of going to, places I had only read about in book and had wondered about. At this stage I was fluent in Italian, the Venetian dialect mainly, but with an excruciating English accent! Friendships with my Italian girlfriends and my Italian relatives became deeper and more meaningful as the years went by.

Eventually, I took Franco home to meet the family in New Zealand. My father thought his surname 'Giacomelli' was actually 'Jack and Smelly', which my father found amusing! Our subsequent move to New Zealand came with huge changes for all of us.

We did adjust in time. Along with the joy of having a property and building our own home, we had the added pleasure of introducing the children to their first dog and the interesting world that accompanies dog ownership. Starting up a new business at the same time did put pressure on us, but by then we knew change and moving forward inevitably brought pressure to bear, but that we could cope with it. Particularly since the option of standing still was not so attractive.

Going back to Venice on holiday is a gift I will always be grateful for as I have been able to maintain the lovely friendships I have made along the way. Over the years we have seen all our friends' children grow up, as ours have. The fact that we could just pick up where we left off from one year to the next with our friends and family who live overseas, has been lovely.

Quite a few of our overseas friends' children were sent out to visit us in New Zealand for stays long enough for them to learn English. We had sent our girls back to visit them in Italy with the same intention, so the situation was reciprocal.

When I was a young woman, about to leave on my overseas experience trip, I remember telling my mother that I would like to write a book. Her reply was that I was doing the right thing. "Travel, see the world, meet interesting people, then you will find the book in you," were her wise words.

Goodness, it has taken a long time!

9781669880479